WILLWRITER

WillWriter Program by Legisoft
WillWriter Manual by Nolo Press

Illustrations by Mari Stein

NOLO PRESS • 950 Parker St., Berkeley, CA 94710

Printing History

Nolo Press is committed to keeping its books up-to-date. Each new printing, whether or not it is called a new edition, has been completely revised to reflect the latest law changes. If you are using this book more than a year or two after the last date listed below, be particularly careful not to rely on information therein without checking it.

Commercial License Information

If you wish to make WillWriter available to the public on your computer, contact Nolo Press for commercial license information.

First Edition   February 1985
Second Printing   April 1985

WillWriter Program: Legisoft (Jeff Scargle
                      and Bob Bergstrom)
WillWriter Manual: Nolo Press (Stephen Elias
                      and Jake Warner)
Illustrations: Mari Stein
Production: Stephanie Harolde and
                      Glenn Voloshin
Book Design: Keija Kimura

ISBN   0-917316-98-3
Library of Congress Card Catalog No.:84-063151

IMPORTANT

PLEASE READ THIS: We have done our best to give you useful, accurate and up-to-date software and written information to help you write your own simple will. But please be aware that laws and procedures in the various states are constantly changing and are subject to differing interpretations. Also, we have no control over whether you carefully follow our instructions or properly understand the information contained on the WillWriter disk or this manual. Of necessity, therefore, neither Nolo Press nor Legisoft makes any guarantees concerning the use to which the WillWriter program or manual is put, or the results of that use. In other words, any will you write using WillWriter is yours and it's your responsibility to be sure it carries out your intentions. If you want a legal opinion regarding the legal effect of any will you write using WillWriter, have it reviewed by an attorney in your state who specializes in wills and estate planning. Also, if you become confused by any aspect of WillWriter or the manual, we recommend you talk to a lawyer before further use.

Nolo Press does offer several services which update all of our self-help law books and software on a regular basis. This includes the Nolo News, a quarterly self-help law newspaper that updates all of our books and software and contains many helpful self-help law articles. In addition, and more specifically, our free WillWriter User's Service provides all registered WillWriter purchasers with notice of any necessary program upgrades and law changes, as well as notification of other Nolo self-help law software as it becomes available, for a two-year period. To receive the Nolo News and the WillWriter User's Service, complete and mail the card found in the disk packet.

Acknowledgements

Many persons--lawyers, programmers and friends--have contributed to WillWriter. The distinctive form and careful legal craftsmanship of the final version owes much to the enthusiastic and knowledgeable support of Steve Elias and Jake Warner of Nolo Press. Daryl McKibbin, Roger Scargle, and Mark Terrel aided in the programming. Carla Holt, Sharon Sittloh, Linda Ross, Deanna Hisaw, Bill Hennessy, Peter Noerdlinger and Steve Nerney contributed to Legisoft in various ways.

It is a pleasure to thank Carol Pladsen and the following people at Nolo Press for their cheerful and enthusiastic production support: Stephanie Harolde, Keija Kimura, Toni Ihara and Glenn Voloshin. Also, we sincerely appreciate the current efforts of Kate Miller, Barbara Hodovan, John O'Donnell, Jack Devaney, Amy Ihara, Stacie Smith and Sue Imperial of Nolo Press in getting WillWriter to the people who will use it.

Finally, we are grateful to the legions who have tested preliminary versions of the program, which led to the discovery of many improvements which would have otherwise gone unnoticed.

Table of Contents

PART 1

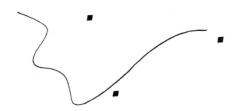

Introduction to Wills and WillWriter

Welcome to WillWriter, a computer program and accompanying manual which permits the average person to efficiently prepare his or her own legal will. WillWriter is designed for use by residents of all states (and the District of Columbia) except Louisiana* to pass all property of the average American adult citizen to family, friends and charities.

WillWriter allows you to make a will with the following options:

---

* Louisiana has several legal rules and procedural requirements different than those called for by WillWriter. If you
live in Louisiana and inadvertantly purchased this program,
please return it directly to Nolo Press and we will promptly
refund your purchase price.

● Leave all your personal property to your spouse,* your children, your grandchildren, your other relatives, your friends or to charity, and divide it among them as you see fit;

● Leave your house and other real estate to your spouse, or children, or to any other person or charity of your choice;

● If you are not married, but live with someone, WillWriter allows you to leave your partner as much of your personal property as you wish, as well as all of your real estate;

● Name a personal guardian to take care of your minor children in case something happens to you and your spouse;

---

* In most common law property states, you must leave your spouse at least a portion of your property either in your will or outside of it. In other states, your spouse has some right to support and to use of the family home. We discuss this in more detail in Part 5.

• If you have no spouse, or are divorced and your spouse does not accept parental responsibility, WillWriter allows you to name a personal guardian for your children in case something should happen to you;

• Name a guardian of your minor childrens' property to serve without bond;

• Leave specific bequests* such as antiques or family heirlooms to particular people or groups;

• Make bequests of cash to family members, friends or charities;

• Include children in your will who were born during an earlier marriage, or when you were not married;

• Name an executor to handle your estate without having to post a bond;

• Specifically exclude a child or children from your will.

Clearly, WillWriter and the accompanying manual enable the user to produce a basic will sufficient for the needs of most adult American citizens and permanent residents, young and old alike. However, some people will want to go beyond WillWriter when planning to dispose of their estate. And, for a very few, WillWriter will be of little value. Let's take a minute to review the types of situations for which the use of WillWriter is either not advised, or its use should be supplemented with other estate planning techniques.

If your anticipated estate is large enough to warrant estate planning (that is, the art of

---

* Here and throughout the rest of the manual we use the word "bequest" to mean any type of property left to specific individuals in a will. Although technically bequests only involve personal property, while "devises" refer to real estate, we use the term here to refer to both types of property. However, in the printed will, we use bequest in its technical sense and refer to real estate gifts as "devises."

keeping your estate taxes and probate fees to the minimum), you should not totally rely on WillWriter for disposing of your property. For these larger estates, you should make a will, but only as part of a more general estate plan which includes limiting the amount of property subject to probate. This might include owning some property in joint tenancy, establishing a living trust, etc. Estate planning is discussed in some detail in Part 6 of this manual. For now, it's enough to realize that if your anticipated estate is worth more than $75,000 or so, you may wish to supplement your will with some estate planning techniques designed to mimimize the value of the property passing through probate. In addition, if your estate, or the combined estate of you and your spouse, is worth more than approximately $600,000,* you will want to familiarize yourself with estate planning techniques designed to reduce taxes. We discuss tax planning in Part 6(C) of this manual.

To sum up, in most situations involving small and medium sized estates, you should be able to safely use WillWriter along with several standard estate planning techniques. One good source of more detailed estate planning information than we can squeeze into this manual is Plan Your Estate: Wills, Probate Avoidance, Trusts and Taxes, by Denis Clifford (Nolo Press). Although the book is written primarily for residents of California and Texas, its discussion of estate planning techniques is valid in other states as well. Once you understand the available ways to minimize the property passing through probate and limit death taxes, you can return to WillWriter and prepare your own will.

Part 9 of this manual provides a number of examples of what can and cannot be accomplished with WillWriter, taking these estate planning considerations into account. Please remember, however, that you are writing your own will and

---

* We use the $600,000 figure because it is the amount that is exempt from federal estate tax for people who die in 1987 or thereafter. The exempt amount in 1985 is $400,000, and $500,000 in 1986.

that WillWriter is only a tool to help you. You
must take responsibility for the result.

   WARNING: If your estate is larger than
$1,000,000, or, if it is smaller and you have
serious questions about estate planning techniques which are not answered by this manual or
Plan Your Estate, it makes sense to use Will-
Writer only as a stop-gap measure until you can
develop a comprehensive estate plan with the
help of a lawyer. Once you reach the million
dollar level, good tax planning becomes both
subtle and tricky and you can and should seek
competent legal and accounting help to supplement your own study of various probate avoidance
and tax-saving techniques.

PART 2

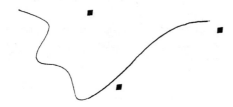

About Wills Generally

The WillWriter program enables you to write your own simple will. Before you begin, however, you may wish to know a little about what a will is and why you need one. As you surely know, the purpose of a will is to insure that your intentions about your property and your minor children are carried out after you die. A will is one way you can officially "speak" after your death.

The laws of the state where the person making the will had his or her home generally govern both the validity of the will and its interpretation. This means that if you make a will in one state and then move to another state, you should review your will, and change it if appropriate. We tell you how to do this in Part 12.

Fortunately, for the purpose of the simple will produced by WillWriter, the laws of most states are basically the same. Because there are some differences, however, WillWriter will ask you to designate your state of residence. Then, when appropriate, you will be presented with information that is specifically relevant to your state. WillWriter will also ask you to specify your county of residence. However, this is done solely for purposes of identification.

The law in almost every state requires you to be 18 or older, and of sound mind, to make a valid will. A few states have slightly different age requirements. We list them here:

Age Requirements to Write a Valid Will

State	Age Qualification to Make a Will
Alabama	19 for real property 18 for personal property
Georgia	14
Indiana	18 or younger if member of armed forces
Iowa	18 or younger if married
Kansas	18 or younger if married
Nebraska	18 or married
New Hampshire	18 or younger if married
Oregon	18 or younger if married
Rhode Island	21, but 18 for personal property
Texas	18, or younger if married
Washington	18, or younger if married to person over 18
Wyoming	19

In addition to the age requirement, you must also be of sound mind to prepare a valid will. The fact that you are reading this manual is some evidence of your mental soundness. However, the usual legal definition of sound mind is that the person making the will:

• Has the capacity to understand the relationship between him- or herself and those persons who would normally be provided for in the will (the "natural objects of his bounty");

• Has the ability to understand the nature and extent of his or her property;

• Has actual knowledge of the nature of the act he or she is undertaking; and

• Has the capacity to form an orderly scheme of distributing his or her property.

If you have any serious doubts of your ability to meet these rules, consult a lawyer.

If you don't leave a will or make some alternative estate plan, the law of each state causes your property to be distributed to your spouse, children or other relatives (if you have no spouse or children) as provided by statute. This is called "intestate succession." And, if you die without a will, you are said to die "intestate."

Dying intestate may be satisfactory for some because the property division mandated by state law is about what they would have done in their will anyway. But, it is generally not a good idea to leave the details of how your property will be divided up to the state. This certainly goes double for all people with children who want to specify someone to care for them should this ever become necessary.

Initially, it would seem to be the easiest of tasks to write a simple will. Why can't you just write something in your own handwriting, such as, "I want my kids to get half of my property, except for the family house, which I want my spouse to have, along with the other half of the rest of my property--except for the gold statuette in the living room, which I want to go to my Aunt Clarissa."* In fact, some states do allow the use of handwritten ("holographic")** wills. Unfortunately, there is often a catch. What you intend by such informal language may not be what your heirs end up with when lawyers finish picking over your words. Consequently, most states require more formal witnessed wills.

Reliance on formal wills, complete with "magic" legal words, isn't necessarily bad. It is a convenient way to make sure you achieve predictable results. It is also true, however, that attorneys have benefited from, and promoted, overly convoluted techniques designed to make people jump through precise (and in some cases, silly) legal hoops in order to control the process of passing money and property from one generation to the next. Some of these hoops (such as probate) are both expensive and avoidable.

In addition to containing at least some formal (magic) words, wills must be signed and witnessed in a ritualistic manner in front of witnesses. The reason for this is fairly obvious. As people become older, they sometimes run the risk of being heavily influenced by friend, relatives and organizations determined to get their property when they die. Requiring a will to be witnessed helps to reduce the risk

---

* The French philosopher Rabelais accomplished the task of writing a one-sentence will, as follows: "I have nothing, I owe a great deal, and the rest I leave to the poor."

** There is a device known as a holographic will which needs not be witnessed. This will must be completely handwritten and signed by the testator to be valid. These types of wills, which are valid in some states but not in many others, are adequate to pass small amounts of property. They are generally considered to be dangerous when it comes to disposing of large assets, however. Why? Because among other things, it is often difficult to establish the authenticity of the decedent's unwitnessed signature after death, giving rise to the possibility that the will may be contested if a lot of property is at stake. Also, as we mention earlier, informal language may not have the result you intend. And finally, because, as we discuss later, wills, whether holographic or not, are generally poor devices to leave large amounts of property.

of coercion and undue influence. Witnesses can
also establish that the person whose name is on
the will really signed it. In many states,
there is also a requirement that the witnesses
be "disinterested"--that is, not receive any
gifts in the will. We discuss witnesses in more
detail in Part 11, Section A.

WillWriter is designed to provide you the
tools and information necessary to do your own
simple will. In doing this, WillWriter follows
accepted procedures and uses necessary "magic
legal words." The program itself and this manual explain all of these in detail. Our goal is
both to have WillWriter help you make a good
legal will and to have you understand the reasons for all the terms and procedures you use.
In addition, we will repeatedly emphasize the
additional steps that many of you will want to
take to maximize the property left to your intended beneficiaries and minimize the amount
collected by the government in estate taxes and
by lawyers in probate fees. This is generally

10

done by limiting the property left by the will
to items of lesser value and disposing of the
large ticket items (e.g., real estate) by alternative estate planning techniques. The more
typical of these techniques suited to moderate-
sized estates are described in Part 6.

PART 3

Computer Wills:
Are They a Good Idea?

At this point, you may be wondering whether computers are really a valuable tool to help you prepare your own will, or if computer wills are just another technological fad. At first blush, wills and computers would seem to have little in common. Traditionally, wills have been associated with rumpled-suited lawyers, antique offices and quill pens, not with the high tech hum of a thinking machine. However, the times are definitely changing. It's not so easy to find a friendly, reasonably-priced family solicitor whom you can trust these days. And, as it turns out, the computer is an ideal tool for assisting you to make a simple will. So helpful, in fact, that a great many lawyers routinely use computers to store many of the same type standardized magic words and phrases that are utilized in the WillWriter program.

Why do computers and wills work together so well for both lawyers and non-lawyers? Fundamentally, **a will consists** of collecting answers to certain **well-defined** questions developed over hundreds **of years.** Doing this isn't difficult once you get to it. Unfortunately for many of us, there is a good deal of initial resistance to overcome when it comes to confronting what will happen when we die. As you probably know, it's easy to put off writing a will until tomorrow, or better yet, the day after. But, once you acknowledge your tendency to procrastinate, and decide to confront it, WillWriter can prove an invaluable aid to writing your simple will.

Like that rumpled-suited lawyer of old, WillWriter's program helps you focus on the questions you must ask to write a sound legal will. Thus, WillWriter asks for information about your property, family and friends, as well as your wishes for disposing of your property, stores your answers, and produces a will tailored specifically to your circumstances. In terms of the questions and answers relevant to the simple will prepared by WillWriter, no attorney, old-fashioned or not, could do better. In fact, when you consider the ease with which you may update your will, the privacy you gain by making your will in your own home, and the money you save in the process, WillWriter offers several advantages as compared to the old lawyer-drawn will. Of course, as we have emphasized several times, you will be wise if you supplement Will-Writer by reading a good estate planning book, such as <u>Plan Your Estate</u>, by Denis Clifford.

How does the WillWriter program work? Once you get it up and operating, it provides you with some introductory messages and explanations on how to interact with the program. (As Part 14 of this manual provides detailed guidance on the computer end of WillWriter, we do not discuss those issues in detail here). After these preliminaries, the fun begins. In a step-by-step process, you are asked to:

1. Provide basic information, such as your name, the state you live in and your spouse's name;

2. Make choices as to whom will inherit your property;

3. Identify the property you want each person or charity to receive;

4. Choose persons who will administer your estate (in legal phraseology, your "executor" or "executrix"); and

5. Choose persons to care for your minor children if this becomes necessary (in legal terminology, this means to appoint your childrens' "guardian").

After you enter each piece of information or answer each question, your answer is displayed on the screen for your verification. In addition, once all appropriate information and your choices have been gathered by the computer, you will be provided another opportunity for careful review of your important responses. Finally, after you have double-checked everything and made any necessary changes, you can direct Will-Writer to print your customized will, ready to sign. The cover sheet to your will tells you what to do next. This, of course, involves signing your will in front of witnesses. We discuss this procedure in detail in Parts 11 and 12 of this manual.

By now you have probably gathered that the WillWriter manual is a crucial part of this package. We implore you to read it before you fire up the program and take it for a spin. While making out a will is not difficult (people managed to do it for centuries before computers were invented), we want you to carefully focus on a number of important considerations. These include making an accurate determination of exactly what is in your estate (i.e., what you own for purposes of leaving it to others in a will), how best to minimize taxes and probate fees, and how best to use wills in the context of a larger estate plan. Please pay particular attention to Part 4, just below, which provides an overview of the rest of the manual, as well as specific recommendations for what parts you should read, depending on your situation.

PART 4

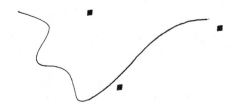

How to Use the WillWriter Manual

The rest of this manual is divided into eleven basic parts, as follows:

Part 5:   What Is in Your Estate?

Part 6:   Estate Planning Basics Designed to Limit Taxes and Probate Fees

Part 7:   Special Considerations for Children

Part 8:   If There is a Problem With Your Will

Part 9:   Sample Uses of WillWriter

Part 10: Checklist For Making Out Your Will

Part 11: Formalities

Part 12: Updating Your Will

This outline incorporates the basic analyti-
cal steps we think you should take before actually writing your will. In other words, your
first task, covered in Part 5, is to inventory
your estate, or "survey your bounty," as the
oylde tyme lawyers used to say. This means
determining not only what you own, but also (if
you are married) separating your property from
your spouse's. It also means determining what
belongs to you but cannot be transferred by a
will, such as property owned in joint tenancy.
Obviously, if you are not married, your job is
easier. For purposes of this manual, it means
you can safely skip Part 5, Sections B and C.

After you have inventoried your estate, you are ready to read Part 6, where we discuss common estate planning techniques designed to minimize the expense and hassle involved in transferring your property to your intended beneficiaries (the people you want to inherit it). Of course, avoiding probate and saving on estate taxes won't help you directly--but it will help insure that your relatives and friends get as much of your property as possible at your death, by avoiding needless payments to governments and lawyers.

Next, in Part 7, we discuss several special considerations that will affect you if you have children. You can skip this section if you are not a parent. If you have children, however, whether they are natural, adopted, or born out of wedlock, Part 7 is essential reading.

Then, in Part 8, we provide some last words about requirements for a valid will and deal briefly with several typical problem areas. This is followed by Part 9, where we provide specific examples designed to illustrate how WillWriter can and cannot be used. This section will be helpful to check your understanding of what you can and cannot do with this program. In fact, you might want to skim Part 9 now to get an idea of the ways in which WillWriter can accomplish your particular goals.

In Part 10, we provide a checklist for making out your will. This provides you with a structured method for considering all the important and necessary choices usually associated with wills. In addition, it should help you determine if you have forgotten any major property or have inadvertently overlooked a person you want included in your will.

Part 11 discusses what to do when your will is complete. This involves the process of signing, witnessing and storing your will. This is important material that everyone should read. Part 12, which alerts you to situations when updating your will is appropriate, is also essential reading.

In Part 13, we give you a brief explanation of each major provision you will find in your will once you print it out. Of necessity, some of these contain some legal gobbledygook, and you will want to be sure you understand exactly what they mean. Indeed, as you read and understand your will line by line, it's even possible that you will be motivated to make changes in the manner we describe in Part 12.

In Part 14, we tell you how to use WillWriter on your computer. This includes both the nuts and bolts of which keys to press and a brief description of what each part of the program is doing in terms of the overall will process. While the WillWriter program can be used without reading this portion of the manual, many readers will prefer to see all the screens in black and white, as well as in green or amber.

Finally, in Part 15, we provide definitions of the legal terminology that appears throughout this manual and in the WillWriter program itself. We encourage you to consult it whenever you become uncertain about the meaning of a particular word or phrase.

Some of you may now be thinking something like this: "Wait, I just want to make a will leaving Aunt Matilda my small savings, my teapot, and the rest of my property, except of course the things I want to leave Uncle George and Nephew Fred. I don't care how much I have, and I don't really want to learn about estate planning."

Others may be thinking: "I only want to appoint a guardian for my kids, not deal with all of my property. Do I really have to go through all of this?"

Our answer to both these questions is "yes." Of course, the less property you own and the simpler your desires, the less important the information in this manual will be to you. Nevertheless, we strongly encourage you to continue. You really do need information on a number of areas, such as how to determine the extent of your property, the effect of your death on your children, probate alternatives, etc., to be able to write an effective will within the context of a sound estate plan. If, despite this admonition, you still want to skip reading what follows and get on with it, we strongly encourage you to also see a lawyer or someone else with sound knowledge of wills. Remember, you are writing your own will and it's your responsibility to learn enough about the process to insure the result will fully meet your needs.

PART 5

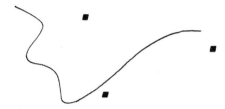

What Is in Your Estate?

Before you actually use WillWriter to help you make your will, you need to know what you own, what it is worth, and what you owe. This is called "determining your net estate." Why is this important? There are two reasons. First, you obviously can't leave property to your loved ones if you don't own it. And, second, before you can think sensibly about using any estate planning devices, you need a good handle on what your property is worth.

For example, if the value of your net estate is over $600,000, you should be seriously concerned about tax planning.* To do this, you will need more specific information and advice

---

* As we mentioned earlier, for deaths that occur in 1987 and thereafter, all property is exempt from federal estate tax up to $600,000. The exemption amount is $400,000 for 1985 and $500,000 for 1986. For simplicity's sake, and because we expect it to be the relevant information for the great majority of readers, we use the $600,000 figure.

than we provide here. You will find this in
Plan Your Estate, by Denis Clifford (Nolo
Press). And, as we said in the introduction, if
your estate is worth more than $1,000,000 or so,
you should almost certainly have your estate
plan reviewed by an expert. But, even if you
conclude you need more help, WillWriter will
generate a good interim will until you get it.

A. Identifying Your Probate Estate

In Section G of this part, you will be asked
to compute the value of your net estate by
listing all your assets and liabilities. (Don't
worry, this isn't difficult.) First, however,
it's necessary to introduce you to the concept
of "probate estate." This is simply the portion
of your total property (your "net estate") which
will be subject to the probate court process
when you die. To say the same thing in a different way, your probate estate is that portion
of your net estate which you pass to relatives,
friends and others in your will.* Also, in the
event you don't make a will, your probate estate
includes the property which is passed to your
relatives under the intestate succession laws of
the state in which you live, or the state in
which your real estate is located.

As we discuss in more detail in Part 6(B),
making sure you only leave a modest amount of
your property by your will is one of the basic
principles of estate planning. Again, the reason for this is simple. Property left in a will
must normally go through probate, and probate
costs money. Because many of the fees (e.g.,
attorney and court fees) involved in the probate

---

* There are exceptions to this rule for very small estates.
State law differs on this point, but many states exempt
property left by will from probate when the total estate is
less than between $30,000 - $60,000. A few states set this
exemption level somewhat higher. In addition, several community property states, including California, allow one
spouse to leave property to the other by will, free of formal
probate.

22

process are established by taking a percentage of the total value of your probate estate, it follows that the more of your property you can leave in ways that avoid probate, the smaller these fees.

Before we go on, let's again emphasize the difference between your "net estate" and your "probate estate," just to be sure you're not terminally confused right here at the beginning. It's simple:

● Your net estate is everything you own minus everything you owe;

● Your probate estate is the total value of that portion of your net estate that ends up dragging through probate, either because you leave it in a will or die intestate.

Figuring out what is in your probate estate is a three-step process:

● First, you catalog everything you own (your net estate);

● Second, you identify the property that for one reason or another will be automatically transferred to someone else upon your death, and therefore outside of probate;

● Third, you deduct the property passed outside of probate from the rest of your property. This is your probate estate.

Basically, the following types of property will not be in your probate estate:

- Real estate (generally termed "real property") held in joint tenancy* (or tenancy by entireties**);

- Joint tenant checking, money market, brokerage or other financial accounts;

- Life insurance;

- Property held in trust, including simple savings bank trusts and living trusts.

See Part 6(B) for more about these probate avoidance devices.

B. Property Ownership Laws

Now that we've pointed out the types of property that pass outside your will and therefore avoid probate, we turn to the important task of cataloging what you own. If you are unmarried, this will be easy. You own what you own, period. If you are married, however, the waters can become as muddy as the mighty Mississippi in springtime. Why? For two reasons. First, your spouse may own some property you believe is in your estate. Second, your spouse may have rights to inherit at least a minimum share of your property, whether you like it or not. In both situations, the laws of your state will determine what is yours to leave by will, and what is not. This means that if you are married (this includes everyone who has not received a final decree of divorce), it's important that you have--or get--some information about:

---

* A joint tenancy is a form of property ownership involving two or more persons where surviving owners automatically inherit the share of a dead owner. Thus, if property is owned by three joint tenants, and one of them dies, the surviving joint tenants split the deceased owner's share 50-50. We discuss this important estate planning concept in much more detail in Part 6, Section B.

** Property held in "tenancy of the entirety" is similar to joint tenancy. Tenancy of the entireties is a somewhat antiquated form of property ownership between husband and wife which exists in about 21 states. Tenancy by the entirety includes the right of survivorship, which means property held in this way does not pass through a will.

• The laws of the state where you are domiciled (permanently living); and

• The laws of any state in which real estate you own is situated.

Fortunately, states can be broadly divided into two types for the purpose of deciding what is in your estate when you die--community property states and common law property states. (See the chart on the next page to identify your state.) Community property states generally presume that property and income received by either spouse during the marriage is jointly owned, whereas common law states do not make this presumption. Both of these approaches are fully discussed in Subsections 2 and 3 just below.

After you refer to the chart to determine the category to which your state belongs, turn to Subsection 2 below if you are married and live in a community property state, and Subsection 3 if you are married and live in a common law state. If you are not married, you can skip to Section D of this part. If while married you moved from a common law state to a community property state (other than California or Idaho), you will need to read both Subsections 2 and 3. Why? Because the property you acquired in the common law state may be governed by one set of rules and the property acquired in the community property state by another. If you move to California and Idaho from a common law state, however, only community property concepts will be used to determine who owns what. We discuss this more below when we talk about moving from state to state.

MARRIAGE NOTE: A surprising number of people do not know whether they are married or not. Problems with making this determination commonly occur in three circumstances:

• Many people have been told, have heard, or somehow believe they are divorced, but have never received any papers to confirm this fact. If you are in this situation, call the court clerk

in the county where the divorce was supposed to
have occurred and get the records. If you can't
track down a final decree of divorce, it's best
to assume you are still married;

• A great many people believe they are married by common law. Most aren't. Common law
marriages can only be formed in the following
thirteen states and Washington D.C.:

Alabama   Montana
District of Columbia   Ohio
Florida   Oklahoma
Georgia   Pennsylvania
Idaho   Rhode Island
Iowa   South Carolina
Kansas   Texas

Do You?
I DO!

AN UNCOMMON-LAW-MARRIAGE

Even in these states, you must intend to be married; merely living together isn't enough to create a common law marriage;

● Some people don't know if their divorce is legal. This is particularly true of Mexican and other out-of-country divorces where only one person participated. This is a complicated area and beyond the scope of this manual. If you have any reason to think that your former spouse might claim to be still married to you at your death, see a lawyer. In the meantime, assume you are still married.

Community Property States

Community Property States	Common Law States
Arizona California Idaho Nevada New Mexico Texas Washington	All other states

---

1. Community Property States

In community property states, what you own typically consists of your separate property and one-half of the property owned as community property with your spouse. Obviously, then, it's extremely important that you know what property falls in the community property category and what is legally classified as your separate property.

a. Community Property

● All employment income received by either spouse during the course of the marriage;*

● All property acquired with employment income received by either spouse during the course of the marriage (but not during permanent separation);

● All property which, despite originally being separate property, is transformed into community property under the laws of your state. This can occur in a number of ways, including one spouse making a gift of separate property to the community (e.g., putting a separately-owned home in joint tenancy), or the spouse with the separate property allowing it to get so mixed together with community property that it's no longer possible to tell the difference (lawyers call this "commingling").

The one major exception to these rules is that all community property states, except Washington, allow spouses to treat income earned after marriage as separate property if they sign a written agreement to do so and then actually keep it separate (as in separate bank accounts). Most people don't do this, but it does happen.

b. Separate Property

* All property owned by either spouse prior to marriage, or property the spouse receives after marriage by gift**or inheritance, as long as you keep this property separate from community property and don't commingle the two. As we

---

* This generally only refers to the period when the parties are living together as husband and wife. From the time spouses permanently separate, most community property states consider newly-acquired income and property as the separate property of the spouse receiving it.
** Community property can be transformed into separate property and vice versa by means of gifts between spouses. Further, one spouse's separate property can be given to the other spouse as his or her separate property. The rules for how to do this differ from state to state.

mentioned, if commingling occurs, separate property may automatically turn into community property.

The community property states differ slightly on what is classified as community property. One of the biggest differences is that in Texas and Idaho, income derived from separate property is considered community property. In California, Arizona, Nevada, New Mexico and Washington, any income earned by separate property is also separate property.

For most couples who have been married a number of years, determining what is community property and what is separate is relatively easy. The lion's share is community, as any property owned before marriage is either gone or commingled. Probably the major exception to this all community generalization is property one spouse receives by gift or inheritance and keeps separate. In some situations, determining whether particular property is separate or community can be more difficult. Here are several potential problem areas:

BUSINESSES: Family-owned businesses can create difficult problems, especially if they were owned before marriage by one spouse and grew later. The basic problem is to figure out whether the growth value is community or separate property. Lawyers approach the problem like this. If both spouses work in the business, then the increase in value which the business undergoes during such period may usually be viewed as community property. However, if only the spouse who originally owned the business as separate property works in it, it is often not so clear whether the increase in value of a business was due to the work of that spouse (community property) or whether the separate property business would have grown anyway. If the latter is true, the increase in value could be separate property in most community property states, except Texas and Idaho.

More succinctly, if you own a family business, it may be difficult for you to distinguish the community property portion from the separate property portion without the advice of an attorney and an accountant. If you plan to leave your share of the business to your spouse, or in a way your spouse approves of, you have no practical problem. However, if your view of who owns the business is different than that of your spouse, and you don't see eye to eye on your estate plans, it's important to get professional help.

MONETARY RECOVERY FOR PERSONAL INJURIES: As a general matter, personal injury awards are the separate property of the spouse receiving them, but not always. In some states, this money is treated one way while the injured spouse is living and another way upon his or her death. Also, the determination as to whether it's separate or community property can vary when the injury is caused by the other spouse. In short, there is no easy way to characterize this type of property. If a significant amount of your property came from a personal injury settlement, you will want to check the specifics of your state's law.

BORROWED FUNDS: Generally, all community property is liable for debts incurred on behalf of the marriage (i.e., the community), while a spouse's separate property is responsible for that spouse's separate debts. Unfortunately, it

isn't always easy to determine whether a particular debt was or was not incurred for the benefit of the community. Further, under some circumstances, a spouse's separate property may be
liable for debts such as food, shelter and other
common necessities of life incurred by the other
spouse. When this is true depends on the law of
each state, as well as the circumstances. The
point is this. It is sometimes difficult to say
what debts the community property (and sometimes
the separate property) left in an estate will be
responsible for. Again, there is normally a
problem only if the spouses disagree.

PENSIONS: Generally, pensions are considered to be community property, at least the proportion of them attributable to earnings during the marriage. However, some federal pensions are not considered as community property because federal law considers them to be the separate property of the employee earning them. At present, Railroad Retirement Benefits and Social Security Retirement Benefits fit within this category. Military and private employment pensions, on the other hand, can be considered as community property.

One question you may be asking at this point is: "So what? If I leave everything to my spouse--what difference does all this information make?" It can make a big difference if you want to keep your probate estate to the absolute minimum. Remember, as we discussed above, all your property (this includes your one-half of community property), along with your separate property, is included in your probate estate* if not placed in joint tenancy, an intervivos trust, or one of the other probate avoidance devices. And remember, too, that the higher the value of your probate estate, the more money your estate must pay in probate fees. However, if particular property is already your spouse's, it is not in your estate at all, probate or otherwise, and you don't need to worry about it. The point, of course, is this: To take full advantage of the probate avoidance techniques discussed in Part 6, it will be most helpful to have a good idea of what you do and do not own.

We include here a chart, called a "Decision Tree," to help you determine what is community property, what is separate property, and what is difficult to classify. Use it like this. First, make a list of all items of valuable property you are not sure whether you own separately or as community property with your spouse. Then follow the chart for each item.

---

* If you do not use any probate avoidance techniques, your net estate and your probate estate will be the same (except that your probate fees will be based on the total or gross value of your property, whereas your "net estate" is measured after your liabilities are deducted from your assets.

Community Property Decision Tree

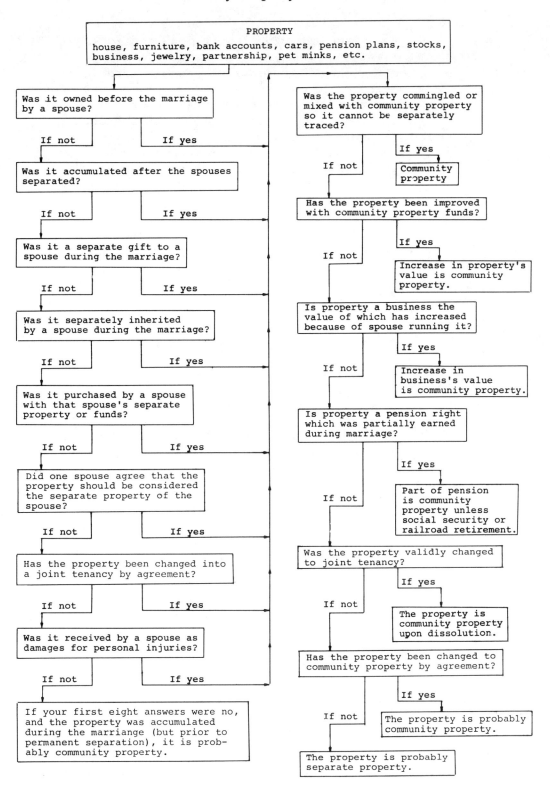

PROPERTY
house, furniture, bank accounts, cars, pension plans, stocks, business, jewelry, partnership, pet minks, etc.

Was it owned before the marriage by a spouse?

If not → Was it accumulated after the spouses separated?

If not → Was it a separate gift to a spouse during the marriage?

If not → Was it separately inherited by a spouse during the marriage?

If not → Was it purchased by a spouse with that spouse's separate property or funds?

If not → Did one spouse agree that the property should be considered the separate property of the spouse?

If not → Has the property been changed into a joint tenancy by agreement?

If not → Was it received by a spouse as damages for personal injuries?

If not → If your first eight answers were no, and the property was accumulated during the marriange (but prior to permanent separation), it is probably community property.

Was the property commingled or mixed with community property so it cannot be separately traced?

If yes → Community property

If not → Has the property been improved with community property funds?

If yes → Increase in property's value is community property.

If not → Is property a business the value of which has increased because of spouse running it?

If yes → Increase in business's value is community property.

If not → Is property a pension right which was partially earned during marriage?

If yes → Part of pension is community property unless social security or railroad retirement.

If not → Was the property validly changed to joint tenancy?

If yes → The property is community property upon dissolution.

If not → Has the property been changed to community property by agreement?

If yes → The property is probably community property.

If not → The property is probably separate property.

2. Examples of Community Property and Separate Property Division

The discussion in the previous section may have left you shaking your head. If so, you aren't alone. Thousands of lawsuits are fought over these issues every year by lawyers who are all supposed to understand them. For most people of good will, however, categorizing separate and community property isn't difficult in most circumstances. Here are some examples to help you and your spouse better understand how community property principles determine what is in your "probate estate."

EXAMPLE 1: You are living in a community property state and your property consists of the following:

• A computer inherited by your spouse during marriage;

• A car purchased prior to marriage;

• A boat which is owned and registered in your name but which was purchased during your marriage with your income;

A family home which you and your wife own as "husband and wife" and which was also purchased with your earnings.

Your net "estate" (all your property) consists of the car, one-half the boat and one-half your equity in your family home. Why? Your car was yours before the marriage and is thus separate property; the boat was purchased with community property income (i.e., income earned during the marriage); and the home was both purchased with community property income and is owned as husband and wife. The computer, on the other hand, was inherited by your spouse and is therefore her separate property. You can leave all the property in your net estate in your will, or you can adopt one or more of the probate avoidance devices discussed in Part 6(B).

EXAMPLE 2: James is married to Sue Ellen. They have three minor children, Peter (15), Sharon (12) and Pilar (10). James and Sue Ellen live in Arizona, a community property state. They own approximately $50,000 equity in a house (with a value of $150,000) as "husband and wife" and a joint tenancy savings account containing $15,000. James separately owns a fishing cabin in Colorado worth $12,000, which he inherited from his father, and an Austin Healy sports car worth approximately $10,000, which he purchased before he was married. In addition, James owns several expensive items received as gifts, including a Leica 35-mm SLR camera ($1,000), a stamp collection ($8,500) and a custom-built computer ($12,000).

NOTE: Remember, gifts or an inheritance received by one spouse after marriage are the separate property of that spouse.

Using WillWriter, James makes the following property disposition:

● His one-half interest in the community property home to Sue Ellen ($25,000, or one-half of the equity*);

● His fishing cabin to Sue Ellen;

---

* James would also be wise to at least consider the several common techniques for transfering valuable property to others outside of a will, and thus outside of probate. It is often particularly advisable to do this with mortgaged real property, because if the property is left by will, the entire value of the decedent's property (in this case, half of $150,000, or $75,000) will be counted when computing probate fees. See Part 6(B).

- His Austin Healy to his brother Bob;*

- His camera to his daughter Sharon;

- His stamp collection to his daughter Pilar; and

- His computer to his son Peter.

James makes no provision for his share of the joint tenancy savings account since this passes automatically to Sue Ellen because of her "right of survivorship."

In addition, James uses WillWriter to appoint his sister-in-law, Karen, as a "personal guardian" for the children in the event Sue Ellen is unable to perform this task. But because Karen is notoriously "loose" when it comes to money, he appoints his father-in-law, Ned, to act as "guardian of the estate" for the children (to handle their property until they turn 18).

3. Additional Resources

As you can see, classification of property as separate or community can be difficult. Indeed,

---

* Joint ownership techniques such as joint tenancy or the use of an intervivos trust can be used for personal property as well as real estate and would accordingly accomplish this same result outside of the will, and thus outside of probate.

it's so convoluted that it has spawned hundreds
of thousands of lawsuits. However, as a general
rule, if you and your spouse agree as to who
owns what property and how you want to dispose
of it, you should avoid any of these legal
hassles. Good sources of information if you are
interested in pursuing this subject further are
Community Property Law in the United States, by
W.S. McClanahan, Bancroft Whitney, 1982; California Marriage and Divorce Law, by Ralph Warner
and Toni Ihara, Nolc Press.

4. Common Law States

Before we plunge into the in's and out's of
property ownership in common law property
states, let us remind you that you really do not
need to know this information unless you are
married. If you are not married, you can leave
all your property as you see fit.

In common law property states, the property
you own consists of:

a. Everything you own separately in your
name if it has a title slip, deed or other legal
ownership document; and

b. If there are no title documents, everything you have purchased with your separate
property and/or separate income. Thus, in these
states the key to ownership for many types of
valuable property is whose name is on the title.
If you earn or inherit money to buy a house, and
title is taken in both your name and your
spouse's, you both own the house. If your
spouse earns the money but you take title in
your name alone, you own it. If title is in her
name, she owns it. If there is no title document to the object as such (say a new computer),
then the person whose income or property is used
to pay for it owns it. If joint income is used,
then ownership is joint (generally considered to

be a tenancy-in-common, unless a written agreement provides for a joint tenancy).*

Let's examine two examples of property ownership rules in common law property states.

EXAMPLE 1: Wilfred and Jane are husband and wife and live in Kentucky, a common law property state. They have five children. Shortly after their marriage, Wilfred wrote an extremely popular computer program which helps doctors diagnose a variety of ills. Wilfred has received annual royalties averaging about $100,000 a year over a ten-year period. During the course of the marriage, Wilfred used the royalties to purchase a car, yacht and mountain cabin, all registered in his name. The couple also own a house as joint tenants. In addition, Wilfred owns a number of family heirlooms, which he inherited from his parents. Over the course of

HARE LOOMS

---

* Despite the general rule stated here, the courts in most states will not allow a manifest injustice to occur. Thus, if property paid for by one spouse ends up in the other spouse's name, the courts will usually find some way (called "using their equity powers") to straighten the matter out so that justice is done. Put another way, the courts will bend over backwards to see that parties only own what they should own.

the marriage, Wilfred and Jane have maintained separate savings accounts. Jane's income (she works as a computer engineer) has gone into her account and the balance of Wilfred's royalties has been placed in his account (which now contains $75,000).

In this situation, Wilfred's property (his net estate) would consist of the following:

• One-hundred percent of the car, yacht and cabin, since there are title documents listing the property in his name. Were there no such documents, he would still own them because they were purchased with his income;

• One-hundred percent of the savings account because it is in his name alone;

• The family heirlooms;

• One-half of the interest in the house.*

EXAMPLE 2: Martha and Scott, husband and wife, both worked for thirty years as school teachers in rural Michigan, a common law state. They had two children, Harry and Beth, both of whom are grown, with families of their own. Generally, Scott and Martha pooled their income and jointly purchased such items as a house, worth $100,000 (in both their names as joint tenants), cars (one in Martha's name, worth $5,000 and one in Scott's, worth $3,000), a share in a vacation condominium, worth $13,000 (in both names as joint tenants), and some of the household furniture. Each maintained a separate savings account (approximately $5,000 in each), and they also had a joint checking account with a right of survivorship, containing $2,000.

---

* Although the house is in Wilfred's net estate, it would go to Jane outside of the estate because of its joint tenancy status. In short, the house is in Wilfred's net estate, but not in his probate estate. However, if the house was in Wilfred's name alone, it would be his property, even if purchased with money he earned during the marriage, or even if purchased with Jane's money.

39

Scott spent several thousand dollars equip-
ping a darkroom he built in the basement. Hop-
ing that son Harry would take up his photography
hobby, Scott placed the entire contents of the
darkroom in a revocable living trust which
passed them to Harry upon Scott's death, but
which left Scott in control during his life.
The remaining property consisted of antiques and
heirlooms which both Martha and Scott had inherited from their respective families.

Scott used WillWriter to make a will leaving
his real estate to Martha and the rest of his
personal property to Beth. After his death,
Martha automatically owned the house and condo-
minium because the property was owned in joint
tenancy, which insured an automatic right of
survivorship. Indeed, where property is in
joint tenancy, as you probably know by now, you
cannot use a will to leave it to anyone other
than the other joint tenant(s).* In other
words, the surviving joint tenant automatically
owns the deceased joint tenant's share free of
probate, and mentioning the property in the will
is redundant and of no legal effect. For the
same reason, the joint checking account with an
automatic right of survivorship went to Martha
outside of the will and free of probate. Harry
received the darkroom equipment outside of probate directly under the terms of the trust.
Beth received Scott's savings account (regardless of the source of the funds) and the specific heirlooms and antiques which were left to
her.**

---

* However, in many states you can unilaterally (by yourself, without permission from the other joint tenant) ter-
minate a joint tenancy prior to death and then leave your
share of the jointly-owned property as you see fit.

** If any antiques were left to Scott and Martha jointly
without specific terms indicating a joint tenancy, Martha
would be entitled to one half of them (or one-half their
value) with the other half going to Beth. This is because
Martha and Scott would have each owned one half of the
antiques as tenants in common, without a right of survivorship.

C. Family Protection in Common Law States

In this section and Section D, we discuss what happens if a surviving spouse is left out of the will or has not otherwise been properly provided for. If you are unmarried, or married and plan to leave your spouse one-half or more of your property in your will, you can skip this discussion and proceed to Section E. Otherwise, read on for important information.

At first glance, it would seem there are few complexities in common law states when it comes to deciding what property you can leave and to whom. If your name is on the title document, or the property was acquired with your funds in the absence of such title, you own it and can leave it by will to the beneficiary of your choice, right? Well, not quite. There is one major problem area. This arises in wills where one spouse attempts to give away all of his or her estate without providing anything to the surviving spouse. Suppose, for example, one spouse owns the house, the car and most of the possessions in his or her name alone and leaves it all to a stranger. The stranger could then kick the surviving spouse out of the house. Of course, this problem does not usually occur, since most people voluntarily give a major portion of their estate to their surviving spouse.

In the event they do not, however, all common law property states have some way of protecting the surviving spouse from being completely, or even substantially, disinherited. While many of these protective laws are similar, they do differ in detail. In fact, no two states are exactly alike.

It takes a bit of history to appreciate why things are so complicated. Hundreds of years ago, the English courts, confronted with the problem of a few people disinheriting their spouses, developed the concept of "dower" and "courtesy." Under dower and courtesy rules, a surviving wife or husband automatically acquired title to a portion of the deceased spouse's real estate by operation of law. "Dower" refers to the interest acquired by a surviving wife, while "courtesy" is the share received by a surviving husband. When the United States was settled, most states adopted these concepts. To this day, all states, except those that follow the community property ownership system (California, Arizona, Texas, New Mexico, Idaho, Washington and Nevada) still retain some version of dower and courtesy.

What specifically happens if the person making the will leaves nothing to his or her spouse, or leaves less than the spouse is entitled to under the law of the state where he or she lives? In most states, the surviving spouse has a choice. He or she can either take what the will provides (called "taking under the will"), or reject the gift and instead take the minimum share called for by the law of the particular state. Taking the share permitted by law is called "taking against the will." In many common law property states, the minimum share that a spouse must receive is one-third to one-half of the property left in the will. The exact amount of the spouse's minimum share often depends on whether or not there are also minor children. In a number of other common law property states, the share that the spouse is entitled to receive is measured by what the spouse receives both under the will and outside of the will. We discuss this concept in Section D, which follows.

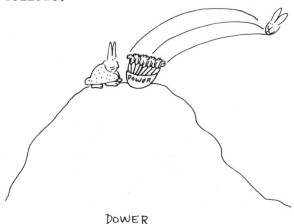

DOWER

When a spouse decides to "take against the will," the property which is taken must of necessity come out of one or more of the gifts given to others by the will. In other words, somebody is going to get shortchanged. You should understand, therefore, that if you do not provide your spouse with at least his or her statutory share under your state's laws, your gifts to others may be seriously interfered with. Put bluntly, if you do not wish to leave your spouse his or her minimum share, and have not otherwise provided for him or her outside of your will, your estate may be heading for a legal mess. It is not wise to let this happen, whether you write your will on toilet paper, use WillWriter or have a lawyer draft your will.

The following chart provides a cursory outline of the basic rights the states give to the surviving spouse. We do not attempt to set out the specifics of every state's law here. Our goal is only to alert you to the problem and to make one point loud and clear. If you wish to substantially disinherit your spouse, see a lawyer before using WillWriter.

Family Protection in Common Law States

I. Surviving spouse receives right to enjoy one-third of deceased spouse's real property for the rest of his or her life (Dower and Courtesy)

Arkansas	Ohio
Connecticut	Rhode Island
District of Columbia	South Carolina
Kentucky	Vermont
Massachusetts	Virginia
Michigan	West Virginia

II. Surviving spouse receives percentage of estate

A. Fixed Percentage

Alabama	1/3 of augmented estate*
Alaska	1/3 of augmented estate
Colorado	1/2 of augmented estate
Florida	30% of estate
Hawaii	1/3 of estate
Indiana	1/3 of estate
Iowa	1/3 of estate
Maine	1/3 of augmented estate
Montana	1/3 of augmented estate
Nebraska	1/3 of augmented estate
New Jersey	1/3 of augmented estate
North Dakota	1/3 of augmented estate
Oregon	1/4 of estate
Pennsylvania	1/3 of estate
South Dakota	1/3 of augmented estate
Tennessee	1/3 of estate
Utah	1/3 of estate
Wisconsin	1/3 of estate

B. Percentage Varies if There Are Children (usually 1/2 if no children, 1/3 if children)

Illinois	North Carolina
Maryland	Ohio
Massachusetts	Oklahoma
Mississippi	Wyoming
Missouri	Minnesota
New Hampshire	Kansas
New York	

C. Other

Delaware ($20,000 or one-third of estate, whichever is less)

Michigan (choice of three options; see Section D, below.)

---

* See Section D below for a definition and discussion of "augmented estate."

III. <u>One year's support</u>

Georgia

D. Property Transferred Outside the Will

Now, suppose you and your spouse agree to several joint ownership and intervivos trust arrangements (see Part 6) which will work to transfer a large part of the estate of the first of you to die to the other. You plan to use your respective wills only to make a series of smaller bequests. Because each of you has already provided for the other outside of your will, you each leave your spouse nothing under the will. After the first of you dies, can the other challenge the will ("take against it") to get one-third to one-half of the property you left in it, even though that person was provided for in other ways? In many states, the answer is "no." The property transferred outside the will is also counted. By way of example, let's look at Michigan.

Michigan has a statute stating that the surviving spouse can select between the following options:

- <u>OPTION 1</u>: The gifts under the terms of the will;

                    or

- <u>OPTION 2</u>: One-half of his/her intestate* share reduced by one-half of the property derived from his/her spouse;

                    or

---

* As mentioned in Part 2, a person who dies without a will is said to have died "intestate." When this happens, there are a whole set of rules in each state about who gets what. The share that someone gets under these rules is their "intestate share." In most states, a surviving spouse's intestate share depends on whether or not there are children. It typically varies between one-third and two-thirds of the probate estate.

- OPTION 3:   Common law dower.*

Now let's return to the example of Scott and Martha discussed above in Section B of this part. You will remember that they put their house and bank accounts into joint tenancy. The result was that Martha inherited nothing under the will, but was well provided for outside it. Now, let's see what Martha could do if she wanted to try and use Michigan law to take against the will or otherwise try to increase her share.

HER SPIRIT IS EVERYWHERE BUN, SON.

WHERE DO YOU SUPPOSE MOM IS PA BUN?

COURTESY

Under Option 1, Martha gets nothing by the terms of the will, but of course still winds up owning all the real estate that was in joint tenancy. If Martha doesn't like this result and elects Option 2, she would get roughly one-third of Scott's probate estate (say $4,000) minus the property she actually "derived" from Scott (i.e., the real estate in joint tenancy). This would come out to less than nothing and is thus not an attractive option. If Martha selected Option 3 instead, she would receive a one-third life estate in the real property. This would be a silly thing to do as she already owns that property by virtue of the joint tenancy arrangement. In other words, because Martha has been

---

* Remember, common law dower is a "life estate" of a portion (usually one-third to one-half) of the real property of the spouse that died.

adequately provided for outside the will, and
this property would be counted in Michigan if
she elects to take against the will, she has no
motive to do so.

Now let's look at a situation where a surviving spouse will benefit from these protections.
For this example, we will use the family protection scheme of the Uniform Probate Code (UPC).
The UPC was proposed in 1972 to simplify probate
law and reduce probate fees going to attorneys.
At present, seventeen states have adopted at
least substantial portions of it, which repre-
sents a heartening trend toward uniformity in
the probate laws. The UPC contains a somewhat
complicated family protection scheme which re-
volves around the term "augmented estate" (note
the number of states in the Family Protection
Chart provided above which use the augmented
estate concept).

The augmented estate, under the UPC, is basically computed as follows:

1. Assess the value of the probate estate
(i.e., the property left in the will which goes
through probate);

2. Subtract the funeral and administration
expenses, and the homestead allowances and exemptions;*

3. Add the sum of a) property transferred by
gift where the total value of the gift or gifts
is worth more than $3,000 and passed outside of
the will during the marriage, but within two
years of the death of the decedent, to persons
other than the surviving spouse, b) property
transferred to persons other than the spouse
that passes at the death of the testator, but

---

* Under the UPC, the surviving spouse is entitled to a
homestead allowance of $5,000. If there is no surviving
spouse, each minor child and each dependent child of the
decedent is entitled to an equal share of the $5,000. If
the state provides for a constitutional right of homestead
in the family home, this value would be subtracted from the
homestead allowance. The UPC also provides $3,500 of per-
sonal property to the surviving spouse or family as exempt
property and a "reasonable" family allowance for one year
(suggested maximum of $6,000).

outside the will (i.e., joint tenancy, living trusts), and c) property transferred to the surviving spouse outside the will. The total is called your "augmented estate." The surviving spouse's elective share (the amount that can be taken against the will) is one-third of this amount.

While the augmented estate concept is complicated (it is probably the most complex part of the UPC--we have even simplified it here a bit), its purpose is clear and easy to grasp. Basically, the surviving spouse is entitled to receive one-third of the net estate rather than the probate estate. This means that in determining whether a surviving spouse has been adequately cared for, the probate court will look to see the value of the property the spouse has received outside of probate, as well as counting the value of the property that passes through probate. This is because authors of the UPC understood very well that people will devise ways to pass their property to others outside of probate to avoid probate fees, as well as by leaving a will.

The following example based on one in the The Uniform Probate Code Practice Manual, Volume 1, published by the American Law Institute and the American Bar Association, should make this clearer.

EXAMPLE: John Abrams, at death, had a joint bank account worth $10,000 with his son Harry. John had created a trust for his daughter Mary, with a value of $60,000. John gave his wife $10,000 worth of stocks during his lifetime. The wife, Charity, invested the stocks, and they are now worth $30,000. John had a $10,000 life insurance policy payable to Charity and a $10,000 life insurance policy payable to daughter Mary.

48

John's probate estate was worth $130,000 when
he died. Charity received a homestead allowance
and exempt property of $8,500 and a family al-
lowance of $6,000. Funeral and administration
expenses and small debts amounted to $15,500.
The will gave Charity $5,000. $10,000 was given
to his brother John, $50,000 to his son Harry,
and the residue of the estate (everything else,
or $35,000) went to daughter Mary.

Let's compute the augmented estate:

1. The probate estate is $130,000;

2. Subtract the various allowances and expenses listed above ($30,000) for a total of
$100,000;

3. To this total add the value of the property passed to others outside the will (bank
account with Harry and the trust for Mary, or
$70,000) and the value of the property Charity
derived from John outside the will (a total of
$40,000). The total augmented estate is
$210,000. Charity is entitled to one-third, or
$70,000. Against the $70,000 is credited first
the $5,000 from the will and then the $30,000
property derived from John and the $10,000 life
insurance. This leaves Charity short $25,000.
Okay, Charity has been given too little. What
happens? Well, assuming she asserts her rights,
someone else loses. The problem of what happens
if there is not enough money to go around is
termed "abatement" and is discussed in more
detail in Part 8 of this manual. Basically,
following the rules of the UPC, all of the other
recipients contribute to the $25,000 (i.e., give
up a share of their inheritance) in equal per-
centages to what they received.

In this case it would work like this. Mary
got $35,000 from the will, Harry got $60,000 and
John got $10,000. Their total is $105,000. So,
Mary gives up 35/105 of the $25,000, Harry con-
tributes 60/105, and John the remaining 10/105.

While the details may be complex, the idea is
simple--if you are living in a state which uses

the augmented estate concept, make sure your spouse is adequately provided for, either under the will or outside of it. If you are living in any other common law state, make sure you either leave your spouse at least one third to one-half of your probate estate in your will or at least enough to satisfy your state's family protection laws. If you don't want to, for some reason, see a lawyer. Also, your spouse should be informed about and agree to your estate plan. This will minimize the chance that he or she will later choose to take against your will.*

E. Moving from State to State

What happens when a husband and wife acquire property in a non-community property state but then move to a community property state? California and Idaho treat the earlier acquired property just the same, as if it had been acquired in the community property state. The legal jargon for this type of property is "quasi-community property." The other community property states do not recognize the quasi-community property concept and instead go by the rules of the state where the property was acquired.** Thus, if you and your spouse moved from any non-community property state into California or Idaho, all of your property is treated according to community property rules (see Section B, above). However, if you moved into any

---

* There are some additional, relatively minor, family protection devices such as "family allowances" and "probate homesteads." These vary from state to state in too much detail for us to discuss here. Generally, however, these devices attempt to assure that your spouse and children are not totally left out in the cold after your death. Accordingly, they should not prove unwelcome to any of you.

** Interestingly, California, Arizona and Texas recognize quasi-community property for dissolution (divorce) purposes. However, Texas and Arizona do not recognize quasi-community property for will purposes, while Idaho does.

of the other community property states from a
common law state, you will need to assess your
property according to the rules of the state
where the property was acquired.

The opposite problem exists when couples move
from a community property state to a common law
state. Here each spouse generally retains their
one-half interest in the property accumulated
while they were married in the community property state. However, the reasoning of the courts
in dealing with the problem has not been totally
consistent. Accordingly, if you have moved from
a community property state to a common law
state, and you and your spouse have any dis-
agreement as to who owns what, you will need to
check with a lawyer.

F. Gifts to Charities

This topic has hung on from times past. It
used to be that gifts to charitable institutions
(e.g., churches, hospitals, educational institutions) could not be made 1) within a certain
time prior to death (e.g., within a year), or 2)
in excess of a certain percentage of a total estate. This was primarily to discourage churches
and other charitable organizations from using
unfair means, such as promising you a place in
heaven, to fill their own coffers at the expense
of a surviving family. While most states have
entirely done away with these restrictions,
seven have not. Consult the following chart.
If you are in one of these states, you should
check with an attorney if you desire to leave a
large part of your estate to a charitable institution, especially if you believe your spouse or
children will object, or you believe you may not
have too long to live.

Restrictions of Gifts to Charities

Time Before Death	Percentage of Estate
(Ranges from 30 days to six months)	(Gift to charity limited to one-third of estate if wife and child are heirs)

District of Columbia (30 days)	Georgia
Florida (6 months)	Mississippi
Georgia (90 days)	
Idaho (120 days)	
Mississippi (90 days)	
Montana (30 days)	
Ohio (6 months)	

TAKING CARE OF FAMILY, FRIENDS & CHARITIES

G. Checklist for Deciding What Is in Your Net Estate

Now that you have an overview of what property you do and don't own, it is time to return to the central point of this chapter, which is to estimate the value of your net estate so you will know what you have to leave and whether estate planning is appropriate. To assist you in this endeavor, we provide a work sheet on the next page. Just put down your best estimates as to what your property is worth--precise numbers are not necessary. You will probably be surprised at the total. Remember, if you and your spouse own community property, only one-half of its value and one-half of any debts owned on it belong to you.

UNCERTAINTY NOTE: When computing your figures, take careful note of those items for which ownership is uncertain. Thus, if you live in a community property state and are unsure whether a $10,000 bank account is community property or your separate property, bear in mind that your net worth figures will be different, depending on how you characterize it. If your conclusion about the value of your net estate depends heavily on characterizations of property about which you are uncertain, you should seek advice from a lawyer or accountant. Otherwise, you may end up leaving property you don't own, or failing to dispose of property which you do.

The Net Value of Your Estate*

I. ASSETS (Add up what you own)

A. Personal Property

 1. Cash _____

 2. Savings Accounts _____

 3. Checking Accounts _____

 4. Money Market Accounts _____

 5. Brokerage Accounts _____

 6. U.S. Savings Bonds _____

 7. Precious Metals _____

 8. Other Bonds _____

 9. Stocks _____

10. Money Owed to You _____

11. Interest in Profit
    Sharing Plan, Stock
    Options, Limited
    Partnerships, Etc. _____

12. Automobiles,
    Boats, etc. _____

13. Household Goods _____

14. Works of Art _____

15. Jewelry and Clothing _____

16. Miscellaneous _____

TOTAL VALUE OF
PERSONAL PROPERTY _____

---

* As you complete this form, it may occur to you that your property, ownership documents and other important papers are spread all over the place. If so, we strongly recommend Your Family Records: How to Preserve Personal, Financial and Legal History, by Pladsen & Clifford (Nolo Press).

B. Real Estate (repeat for each piece of prop-
    erty you own)

Current Market Value   _____

C. Business/Property
    Interests

Value of any Partnership,
Sole Proprietorship, Share
of Small Corporation You
Own   _____

D. Value of Any Patents,
    Copyrights, and
    Royalties   _____

E. Value of Life
    Insurance* (face
    value minus amount
    borrowed, if any)   _____

F. Value of living
    trusts and bank
    account Totten
    trusts   _____

TOTAL VALUE   _____

TOTAL THE VALUE OF ALL
THE ASSETS LISTED ABOVE   _____

II. LIABILITIES (add up what you owe)

A. Mortgage debts
    (include all money
    you owe on real
    property listed
    above   _____

---

* REMEMBER: If you have a term policy, the term may expire
before you die, leaving the people you named in the policy
nothing.

B. Personal property
    debts: (loans,
    total car payment
    obligations, other
    debts   _____

C. All taxes owed   _____

D. Any other liabilities   _____

TOTAL   _____

III. NET WORTH (subtract what you owe from
      what you own)

FROM TOTAL ASSETS: _____

SUBTRACT TOTAL
LIABILITIES: _____

NET ESTATE   _____

MR. AND MRS. BUN'S BOUNTY

PART 6

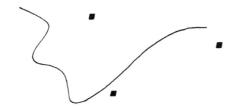

Estate Planning Basics

A. Overview

As we mentioned in Part 1, because of its simplicity most people can safely use WillWriter to make their own will without the assistance of an attorney (except for a final review, if desired). However, let us again emphasize that making a will is not the only thing a wise person will do in preparation for that inevitable day. Although everyone should have a will, it is generally desirable to limit or reduce the amount of your property which is to be passed by it. Why is this? Because, as we have mentioned several times, leaving a large amount of property by will (or by intestate succession) results in your estate being subjected to probate (a formal court procedure through which your estate is distributed). This, is turn, often means long delays, as well as significant probate fees.

Practically speaking, the probate process means it will take six months to a year or more for your heirs to receive your property. Also, lawyers will be paid handsomely to accomplish tasks that are not usually necessary. In most states, however, a certain amount of property, usually in the $30,000 - $60,000 range, can be left by will (or by intestate succession) either free of probate or subject only to a simple, informal do-it-yourself probate process.* In addition, many states simplify or eliminate probate for property left by one spouse to the other. This generally means that if you do not have property of great value, and plan to use WillWriter only to leave small bequests of money and personal property, you need not worry much about the probate avoidance techniques discussed in Section B of this part. Similarly, you will not face any federal estate taxes, so you can also skip Sections C and D and go on to Part 7.

As far as federal estate taxes and state inheritance taxes are concerned, choosing to transfer your property outside of a will can result in tax savings if you are willing to give up ownership or control of your property prior to your death. We discuss this in Section C of this part.

Your next question is probably something like this: "If a will puts property into the probate system and may result in higher estate taxes, why have one at all?" There are a number of reasons. Important among them are:

• If your estate, combined with that of your spouse, is of medium size (up to $600,000), federal tax planning is not necessary because your estate will be obligated for little or no tax. See Section C below for more on this;

• If your estate is modest (in the $30,000 - $60,000 range, depending on state law) the elimination of probate or simplified probate procedures substantially reduce the need to pass property outside of your will. As mentioned,

---

* In a few states, this amount is slightly higher.

58

some states also do away with the need for probate for property left by one spouse to the other;

• Even if you have provided for your property by some means other than a will, you may end up owning valuable property shortly before death. So, for this reason alone, a will is extremely valuable to back up other estate planning devices;

• A will is an easy way to make a quick estate plan which can be elaborated on later, as you get more property; and

• A will allows you to name a guardian for your children and an executor for your estate.

To sum this up, avoiding probate, saving money on taxes, and making a will are the three basic aspects of "estate planning." If you have a medium-sized estate, you will want to at least seriously consider avoiding probate and making a will. If your estate is small, however, just making a will is usually sufficient. If your estate is over $600,000, or, if you are married and the combined estate of you and your spouse is over $600,000, you will also want to think about several ways to reduce federal estate taxes.

In the next several pages we will summarize the common techniques used for probate avoidance and estate tax reduction. Please realize, however, that of necessity we only provide an overview. A good source of more sophisticated information on this area is Plan Your Estate: Wills, Probate Avoidance, Trusts & Taxes, by Denis Clifford (Nolo Press), a thorough book that everyone with even a moderate-sized estate should read. Although published in two editions, specifically for California and Texas, the general information it contains on estate planning is of value everywhere.

B. Probate Avoidance

1. Introduction

The purpose of probate avoidance is quite
obviously to minimize the amount of property
which must pass through a court supervised probate proceeding after your death. This means
passing all or most of your property by one or
more safe devices other than a will. As you
should know by now, property disposed of by the
will becomes subject to "probate" unless its
total value is within the amount made exempt
from probate by the law of your state. In
addition, some states, such as California, allow
one spouse to leave property to the other free
of probate, no matter what the amount. So, if
you plan to leave all, or most, of your property
to your spouse, you should check if probate will
be required in your state. If not, you don't
need to worry about probate avoidance techniques.

Much of the expense of probate results from the fact that the fees of the attorney who takes your estate through the probate court will be a fixed percentage of the probate estate's value. In some states, further, the fees are computed from the estate's total market value. Thus, if the market value of your estate (which is subject to probate) is $900,000, the attorney's fees in some states will be based on the $900,000 figure. This is true even if your equity (the amount you actually own) in the property is much less, say $500,000. Although the percentages vary from state to state, probate fees can devour a modest but significant chunk of your estate, to the detriment of your heirs. These fees are commonly an outrageous amount to pay for simply transferring property to close family members and friends, especially in situations where no one is disputing the will. Also, once an estate goes into probate, it can be extremely slow to come out, with common delays of a year or more before your heirs get all of the money or property you leave them. Many probate avoidance techniques are simple. Let's take a closer look at some of these.

NOTE: Probate avoidance techniques pay big dividends in the form of saving on probate fees, but they obviously only do this at your death. Unfortunately, some of them involve at least some trouble to set up (e.g., savings bank trusts), while others actually involve your giving up control over some or all of your property (e.g., gifts and joint tenancy). Accordingly, many younger people rely primarily on a will to dispose of their property should they die unexpectedly and wait to make a probate avoiding estate plan until they are older and more settled. See Plan Your Estate by Denis Clifford for detailed instructions about how to set up all of the common probate avoidance techniques.

2. Living or Intervivos Trusts

This is an arrangement under which title to property is transferred by its living owner (called a "trustor") to a person or institution (called a "trustee") to hold for a third person (called a "beneficiary") until one or more specified events happen. In a revocable living or intervivos trust, the trustor (the owner of the property) and the trustee are the same person. This allows the owner of property to put it in a trust completely controlled by him or herself. The trust can be revoked by the trustee at any time for any (or no) reason. Thus, the owner continues to enjoy the full use of the trust property during his or her life and can even end the trust, sell the property, and spend the money at the races if he or she chooses. At the owner's death, the living trust device allows the property to be passed to the named beneficiary(ies) under the terms of the trust instrument (the written document establishing the trust) and thus outside of probate.

EXAMPLE: James wants to leave his valuable painting collection to his son, but wants total control over it until he dies. He doesn't want the value of his collection, $500,000, included in his probate estate. To do this, he establishes a revocable (i.e., he can change his mind and snatch the money back) living trust for the paintings, naming himself as trustee while he lives, with his son the beneficiary. When James dies, his son receives the paintings outside of probate. However, should James want to sell a painting, or all the paintings, and end the trust before he dies, he can do so.*

---

* To the extent that you are young and therefore more uncertain about what property you will be leaving when you die, living trusts are excellent devices for keeping property out of your probate estate and yet retaining total flexibility over it while you are living.

Now, assume James also wants to save on federal estate taxes and wants to know if a revocable living trust will accomplish this goal. No. Living trusts will not reduce death taxes at all. By and large, all property over $600,000 is taxed by the federal government at your death, whether or not it goes through probate. There are several ways that people with larger estates can save on taxes, but they generally involve fully surrendering control of the property prior to death (see Section C, below).

3. Joint Tenancy

Joint tenancy is ownership of property by two or more people under terms that automatically pass title of an owner who dies to the surviving owner or owners.* This "right of survivorship" means that the share of one joint tenant automatically passes to the other(s) upon death, outside of the probate process. While joint tenancy is an excellent probate avoidance technique when you are relatively certain about who you want your property to go and don't reasonably anticipate a change of heart, it is not as flexible a device as the irrevocable trust discussed above, since by placing your property in a joint tenancy, you are giving the other joint tenant equal ownership.

Okay, now that you know what joint tenancy is, how do you tell if you own property in joint tenancy? Well, if it is real estate you are concerned with, look at the deed. If it says: "To John Jones and his wife Sarah, in joint tenancy," or "As joint tenants," it's clear. If the deed says, "To John and Arthur Jones as tenants-in-common," then it's just as clear that

---

* In some community property states such as California, married couples may prefer to hold their property "as community property." This is because community property passes to the surviving spouse outside of probate at the same time that both the decedent's and the survivor's share of the community property is automatically eligible for a stepped up tax basis. See Clifford, Plan Your Estate, for more details.

you are not joint tenants. Why not? Tenancy-
in-common is another traditional form of co-
ownership which does not have rights of survivorship. A tenant-in-common can, and should, use
a will or other estate planning device, such as
a living trust, to dispose of his or her share
of such property, since it won't pass automatically upon his or her death.

JOINT TENANCY

What if your deed says, "To John and Arthur
Jones"? This is one of the most frequently
asked law school questions. The answer is that
most states presume a tenancy-in-common on the
reasoning that if the co-owners wanted to create
a right of survivorship, they surely would have
said so in the deed. (Welcome to the world of
judicial reasoning!) However, if the persons on
the deed are married, community property states
do not engage in this presumption. Rather, the
property will be treated as community property.
What this means, and how you can tell whether
you are in a community property state, was covered earlier, in Part 5(B).

Can personal property (all property that
isn't real estate) be held in joint tenancy?
Yes, so long as there is a written contract to
that effect. Joint tenancy bank accounts, for
example, require a written form which is signed
by the joint tenants and which specifies the
account as a joint tenancy. If you don't know
whether your joint account fits this description, ask the bank.

4. Totten or Savings Bank Trusts

These are a very simple type of living trust where the trustor opens a bank account (e.g., checking, savings, certificate, or bank money market) in her name in trust for a named beneficiary. Again, the original owner of the money going into the account (the trustor) retains complete use of the money until her death, at which point any money left in the account belongs to the named beneficiary. If all the money has been withdrawn prior to death, the beneficiary gets nothing. If you want to establish this type trust, simply visit your bank and add a "pay on death" designation to your accounts.

5. Gifts

Property given away when living is not part of the probate estate upon death. For property to be considered a gift, the person giving it needs to actually surrender ownership and control of the property while he or she is living.

6. Life Insurance

Assuming that you designate a specific beneficiary in your life insurance policy, as is usually done, the proceeds of the policy pass under the terms of the policy rather than under probate. Accordingly, the purchase of life insurance policies is a popular way to avoid probate. However, if for some reason a person designates his or her estate as the beneficiary of the policy, which is rarely done, the proceeds would then be part of the probate estate.

7. How Much Is Your Probate Estate?

At this point, you may wish to figure out the value of your property that will pass through probate, assuming you make a will to cover all the property not already taken care of by one or another of the probate avoidance devices. Here is how to do it.

First, turn back to the chart at the end of Part 5, Section G, where you computed your net estate. Simply recalculate your total estate by using the market value for all the items you still owe money on. In other words, value your house, car, land in the country, and boat as if you owned them free and clear. This number, which will be larger than the amount you arrived at for your net estate, unless you don't owe any money, is your "maximum potential probate estate" (i.e., potentially used as the basis for computing your probate fees, depending on your state), unless you have adopted one or more probate avoidance devices. If you have, subtract the market value of all items that will pass outside of probate from your maximum potential probate estate to determine what will actually go through probate.

Most people will find themselves subtracting one or more of the following items from their maximum potential probate estate:

• The pay-off value of your life insurance policies, unless you decide to designate your estate as the beneficiary (very rarely done);

• The value of any real or personal property held in joint tenancy;

• The value of any property covered by a living trust; and

• The value of any property in a "Totten" (savings bank) trust.

Again, the result of this calculation is your "actual probate estate."

66

If this amount is enough to cause probate fee problems in your state (generally about $30,000 to $60,000, depending on the state, with some states exempting all property left to a surviving spouse), you should consider what additional property, if any, can easily be removed from your probate estate so that your probate fees will be minimized. As mentioned, a living trust is often a good way to accomplish this, especially if your age or property ownership situation requires more, rather than less, flexibility.

EXAMPLE: Walter Jackson's estate consists of:

1. $10,000 in savings;

2. A house worth $150,000, with a $75,000 mortgage;

3. A car worth $8,000, on which he owes $4,000;

4. A stamp collection worth $25,000.

Applying the approach used in Part 5(E), we can quickly determine that Walter's net estate is $114,000. To compute his "maximum potential probate estate," however, we have to use the full market value of his property, not the amount he owns. Figured this way, Walter's probate estate would be $193,000, unless he adopts one or more probate avoidance techniques. If Walter put his house in joint tenancy or a living trust, for example, it would pass outside of probate and his actual probate estate would be $43,000. In many states, this amount would be exempt from probate altogether.

C. Tax Reduction

1. Introduction

At death, all property owned by you is subject to a federal estate tax (and state inheritance or estate taxes, if your state has these so-called death taxes), unless it is exempt from taxation. This is true not only for property passed by your will, but also for property passed at death outside of probate, such as property in joint tenancy or in a living trust or savings bank trust. Only if you have actually surrendered control over your property, as well as title to it, prior to death will the taxing authorities consider it as being non-taxable as part of your estate.*

One primary goal of estate planning is to either reduce the amount of property which you leave at death, by giving it away before you die, or to leave property in a way that results in the minimum possible taxation. There are a number of methods for accomplishing this for large estates--$1,000,000 or more--and several commonly used ones for estates of moderate size. We discuss only the latter here. As we have stressed earlier, if your estate is in the $1,000,000 class, you will be wise to invest a few of those dollars in a consultation with a tax attorney or accountant, or both.

Before we review common estate tax-saving techniques, let's consider whether such planning is necessary for your estate. Fortunately, as of 1985, there is no federal estate tax for estates with a net worth of $400,000 or less. This amount increases to $500,000 in 1986, and $600,000 in 1987. Again, as noted earlier, we use the $600,000 figure throughout this text for the sake of convenience. If your anticipated estate is less than these amounts, and you have not given away large amounts of property while

---

* Gift taxes are basically the same as estate taxes except you may give away $10,000 per person per year free of any tax.

living, you do not need to worry about how to
reduce federal taxes. If, on the other hand,
either your estate alone, or the combined value
of your own and your spouse's estate (in common
law property states) is expected to be larger
than these amounts, then creative thought as to
how to reduce your taxes is warranted.

What about state inheritance taxes? A number
of states don't have any. And many that do exempt the same or even larger amounts of property
than does the federal government. Inquire of
your state's taxing authorities for the rules
that affect you.

If you do anticipate estate tax liability
(whether federal or state), however, you should
be aware, at the very least, of the common ways
to reduce or eliminate it. Let's take a closer
look at some of these.

2. Gifts

One way to reduce your estate and save on
estate taxes is to transfer your property while
you are still alive. You may give $10,000 to
any person free of gift taxes each year. Your
spouse may do the same. Thus, if a couple has
three children, they could each give $10,000 to
each child each year, thus transfering $20,000

free of federal gift tax per child and removing
this amount from their estate. In ten years, a
total of $600,000 could be transferred in this
way tax free. Indeed, this would probably result in your saving a much larger sum because of
the interest and dividends this money would earn
which would, absent a gift, have ended up in
your estate. With a gift, the interest and
dividends will instead be earned by the people
to whom you give the money and whom, presumably,
are in a much lower income tax bracket.

If you are planning to give a substantial
gift to a minor, you should investigate using
the Uniform Gifts (Transfers) to Minors Act
discussed in Part 7(E).

3. Testamentary Trusts

There are a number of ways that irrevocable
trusts can be used to save taxes. These do not
include revocable living trusts, under which you
do not give up control of the property in the
trust. To save taxes, a trust must involve a
complete surrender of ownership and control over
the property placed in it. Two of the simpler
ways to accomplish this involve:

● Having each member of a married couple set
up a trust with their children or other loved
ones as the ultimate beneficiaries and the surviving spouse receiving the trust income during
their life. This is an alternative to each
spouse leaving money to the other outright and
paying a hefty estate tax on the combined property when the second spouse dies. For more on
this, see the marital deduction note below.

● Establishing a trust for the benefit of
grandchildren (with the income to go to your
children during their lives) instead of leaving
the money directly to the children and having
them pass the money along when they die. Under
a special Internal Revenue Code provision, your
estate pays an estate tax when you die, but no

70

additional tax is owed when the children die and
the grandchildren get the money. However, only
$250,000 per child (not per grandchild) can be
passed in this way. Obviously, establishing
this sort of trust only makes sense if you have
a considerable amount of money you don't need
and your children also have enough that they can
get along without it.

EXAMPLE: If you have nine grandchildren but
only three children, you can put $750,000 in
three trusts of $250,000 each, with the money to
be ultimately divided among your grandchildren.
Your children receive the income from the trust
during their lives, and your grandchildren get
it without a second estate tax bite.

TAX PLANNING NOTE: There are all sorts of
trusts and all sorts of ways clever accountants
and lawyers have found to reduce the tax bite on
very large estates. Again, if you have more
than $1,000,000, you have enough to hire one of
them to advise you.

D. The Marital Exemption

All property transferred from one spouse to
another at death is exempt from federal (and
usually state) estate tax. This is true even if
you leave far more than the $600,000 amount
which is exempt from tax from 1987 on. Even so,
it may not be wise to transfer a large estate to
an elderly surviving spouse. Why? Because if
the survivor has property of his or her own, and
that property, combined with what you leave, is
worth more than $600,000 in 1987, a large and
unnecessary estate tax will have to be paid when
the second spouse dies.* The larger the estate,
the steeper the graduated tax rate. In this
situation, there will be far less total tax
liability if the first spouse left all the property, or a portion of it, directly to the chil-

_____

* Estate taxes begin at the relatively high rate of 37% of
all property that is not exempt. As of 1987, $600,000 of
property is exempt from all federal tax.

dren, or established a trust with the surviving spouse getting the income, but the principal going to the children or other object of his or her affection.

   EXAMPLE: Suppose Calvin and Phyllis, husband and wife, each have an estate worth $450,000. Calvin dies in 1987, leaving all his property to Phyllis. Because of the marital exemption, no estate tax is assessed. Phyllis dies in 1988. Her total estate is the entire $900,000, which she leaves to the children. In 1989, since $600,000 can be left to anyone free of estate tax, $300,000 of the money left to the children is subject to tax. Unfortunately, however, the rate at which it is taxed under federal estate tax law is the rate for $900,000 (39%).

   Now, suppose Calvin had not left his property to Phyllis, but directly to his children. In this situation there would be no tax liability since when Calvin died (in 1987) he could transfer his $450,000 to anyone free of estate tax. Likewise, when Phyllis died in 1989, she could transfer her $450,000 to the children free of estate tax.

E. Estate Planning Summary

   For people with relatively modest amounts of property (say $30,000 - $60,000 or less), a will adequately solves all their estate planning problems because their estate will neither be subjected to federal estate tax nor probate fees. For somewhat larger estates, consideration should be given to passing property outside of probate to minimize probate fees and delays. People with large estates will find that estate planning involves both making a will and reducing the amount of taxable property passed by it. The more an estate is worth, the more important estate planning becomes. As noted above, even though you will probably want to limit the property you pass by your will, you still need one.

PART 7

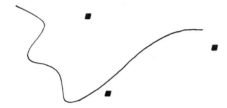

Children

A. Taking Care of Children After Your Death

This part is only for those readers who have children. Among the most pressing concerns of parents with minor children is what will happen to the children in the event the parents die. Here are the general rules. If there are two parents willing and able to care for the children, and one dies, the other parent will generally take over physical custody and control and may (but is not necessarily required to, in most states) carry out the wishes of the other parent in respect to any property left to the children. But, what about situations where both parents are killed simultaneously, or you are a single parent and the other parent is dead, missing, or (you believe) unable to care properly for the children? Who will care for the children after your death? Or, if you are leaving property to the children and the other parent doesn't have sound money sense, who will see to it that the property is conserved for the children's best interests and not squandered unwisely?

The will produced by WillWriter recognizes these concerns and has several features which are designed to meet them. Using WillWriter, you can:

● Name a personal guardian for your children. This person will be appointed by the probate court to act as a surrogate parent for your children if: 1) the court handling the probate of the will finds him or her fit to assume such responsibilities, and 2) no surviving natural or adoptive parent is able to properly care for the children. Unlike natural and/or adoptive parents, a stepparent is not necessarily presumed to be the best guardian for the children. Accordingly, if your spouse is a stepparent to your children and you desire him or her to be the guardian, you should definitely say so in your will.

EXAMPLE 1: Ariadne names her sister, Penny, to serve as personal guardian in the event that her husband, Ralph, dies at the same time as she does or is otherwise unavailable to care for the children. As it turns out, Ralph and Ariadne die in a plane crash. Ralph's mother wants custody of the children, but the probate court appoints Penny, since no evidence has been introduced which would prevent her from serving as the children's legal guardian. If Ralph's will had named his mother, however, then the probate court would have to choose between Penny and Ralph's mother. The lesson of this is clearly that Ralph and Ariadne should communicate and name the same person, if possible.

EXAMPLE 2: Susan and Fred, an unmarried couple, have two minor children. Although Susan loves Fred, she doesn't think he is capable of raising the children on his own. She uses Will-Writer to name her mother, Elinor, as personal

guardian. If Susan later dies, Fred, as the
childrens' natural parent, will probably be
given first priority over Elinor if the court
finds he is willing and able to care for the
children. If, however, the court finds it is
not in the childrens' best interest to have Fred
as their guardian,* Elinor would get the nod,
assuming she was fit. Also, if Fred was not the
natural father, but only the stepfather, Elinor
would probably be named as the guardian if Susan
had named her in the will.

GUARDIAN FOR YOUR HARES

EXAMPLE 3: Now let's change a few facts and
assume that Susan and Fred live together with
Susan's minor children from an earlier marriage
or relationship. The natural father is out of
the picture, but Susan fears that her mother,
Elinor, will try and get custody of the kids if
something happens to her, partially because

---

* In some states, including California, a natural parent is
entitled to custody unless the court finds the children
would actually be adversely affected.

Elinor doesn't approve of anyone who would "live in sin." Susan wants Fred to have custody because he knows the children well and loves them. She should use WillWriter to name Fred as personal guardian. Should something happen to Susan, and Elinor goes to court to try and get custody, the fact that Sue named Fred will give him a big advantage. And, if he is in fact a good parent, he will probably prevail in most states.

● Name a guardian for your childrens' property. If you are leaving a significant amount of property to your children and you think the personal guardian whom you named is not a good money manager, you can name a separate guardian (called "guardian of the estate") to control the property until your children become adults.*

EXAMPLE: Ralph and Ariadne agree that Ariadne's sister, Penny, would be best at caring for the kids, but that Ralph's mother should handle the property until the kids become adults and are able to handle it themselves. Accordingly, in both of their wills, they name Penny as personal guardian and Ralph's mother as guardian of the estate.

● Give specific bequests of money or other personal property to individual children. WillWriter allows you to leave specific items of personal property to specific children. This will assure that your actual wishes as to which children should receive which property will be carried out after your death.

---

* If you wish to name a bank or other financial institution, check with them as to their rules, fees, etc. Many are not interested in small estates. Also, some courts might balk at allowing a division between the personal and financial duties of a guardian. Further, the court will probably refuse to appoint a guardian of the estate when a natural parent has custody over the child. In these situations, the natural parent, or the person you have named as personal guardian, will assume the financial duties as well.

● Leave equal shares of all your real property to your children.

WARNING: WillWriter does not allow you to leave individual pieces of real property to individual children (i.e., your house to one child and your ski lodge to another), or different percentage shares of your total real property to different children (i.e., 50% of your real estate to one child and 25% to the other two). Nor does WillWriter assist you in setting up a testamentary trust for the benefit of the children. WillWriter does not allow for this level of complexity at least in part because we feel many people will choose to use one or more probate avoidance devices to pass their real estate and will therefore not be including it in their will.

B. Pretermitted Heirs

There are special rules regarding children (and children of a deceased child) who are not mentioned or provided for in a parent's will. Most states have rules protecting children, and in some cases grandchildren, from being accidentally disinherited. It's not that you can't exclude a child or grandchild from your will if you wish. You can. It's simply that laws are on the books in most states to make sure you really intended to do it. Although the specifics vary somewhat from state to state, the general rule can be stated as follows: If your will fails to either mention or provide for one or more children, or the children of a child who has died before you (called a "predeceased child"), such children and/or grandchildren may inherit anyway. In addition, the laws of most states protect children who are born after the making of the will but prior to your death (called "afterborn children") by also giving them an automatic share of your estate. In legalese, this entire group is called "pretermitted heirs."

Heirs who qualify as being accidentally over-looked, or afterborn, inherit the share of the estate which they would have received had you died intestate--that is, without a will. It may be fine for pretermitted heirs to receive a share of your probate estate if you really did forget to include them, but it can play havoc with your intentions if you didn't mention them precisely because you did not wish them to in-herit anything.

For example, assume you leave your house and most of your property to your spouse, with sel-ected items going to your three children. If one of your children dies, leaving children of his or her own, and these children (your grand-children) are not specifically mentioned and/or provided for in the will, they may be able to inherit individual shares of their own. This would result in your spouse and your remaining two children receiving proportionately less than you originally intended.

Fortunately, this pretermitted heir problem is easy to protect against. WillWriter asks you to name all your living children, whether natur-al, adopted or born out of wedlock (see Section D below if this applies to you), and all living children of any child who has previously died (see Section C, below). Each of these named children, or grandchildren if a child is de-ceased, will then be listed in your will as receiving $1.00 in addition to any other proper-ty you specifically leave to them (e.g., real estate, personal property, cash, etc). By nam-ing all children and all children of any de-ceased child, and providing each with a minimal inheritance of $1.00, you protect your estate against the "pretermitted heir" problem, even if you leave the particular child or grandchild nothing else. On the other hand, as mentioned, if you use WillWriter to leave all or any of your children (or grandchildren of a deceased child) property in addition to the automatic $1.00 gift, they simply get what you leave them, plus a $1.00 bonus.

This protective device will work extremely

well if you update your will in the following two situations:

1. If one of your children dies before you and leaves children of his or her own, you should redo your will, at least to the extent that you list these grandchildren, so that they will receive $1.00 (of course you can leave them more if you wish). If you fail to do this, these grandchildren may qualify as pretermitted heirs and be able to challenge your will and take a share of your estate.

2. If a child is born to or legally adopted by you after you make your will, you should change your will to provide for such new child. If you don't, that child may qualify as a "pretermitted heir" and sue to receive a share of what you leave. See Part 12 on how and why to keep your will up to date.

EXAMPLE 1: Todd is married and has one child, Millie, when he makes his will. His will leaves one-half of the estate to his spouse and one-half to Millie. Several years later, Todd fathers two additional children, but forgets to make a new will or amend the old one (execute a formal change known as a "codicil") to mention them as well. In most states, the two additional children (called "afterborn" children) would qualify as being accidentally overlooked (pretermitted heirs), since they were not mentioned in the will. This means that at Todd's death, the two afterborn children will be entitled to the share of Todd's probate estate they would have received had Todd not left a will.

EXAMPLE 2: Now, let's change a few facts and assume that Todd wrote his will after all three children were born, but only left property to two of them, intentionally failing to mention the third because of family differences. Again, in most states, the unmentioned child would inherit the same amount he or she would have been entitled to if there were no will.

EXAMPLE 3: Now assume that Todd uses Will-Writer and lists Millie's name but does not designate her to receive any of his personal or real property. By listing Millie's name, Todd automatically tells WillWriter to give her $1.00 in his will. This takes care of any pretermitted heir problem that might exist in respect to Millie. Millie gets the dollar, but no more.

C. What Happens if Beneficiary Fails to Survive

What happens if a person named in your will to receive a bequest fails to survive you by 45 days, and you have not updated your will to account for this fact? Who gets the property? WillWriter produces different results, depending on which of the following situations apply.

1. Specific Bequests to Children

If you make a specific bequest of personal property to one or more of your children without naming an alternate(s), the bequest passes to that child's children (your grandchildren). If you name an alternate(s), then the alternate gets the bequest.

Example: Janie makes out a will leaving most of her estate to her husband and certain specific family heirlooms to their child Ellen. Ellen fails to survive Janie by 45 days, but leaves three children of her own. If Janie named her husband as an alternate beneficiary of the heirlooms, then he would get them. If Janie failed to name an alternate, the grandchildren would inherit the heirlooms in equal shares.

2. Specific Bequests to Beneficiaries Other than Your Children

If you make a specific bequest of personal property to anyone other than your children, and you have not named an alternate(s), the bequest passes to your "residuary estate" (i.e., it goes to those named to receive the "rest of your property". If you name an alternate(s), then the alternate gets the bequest.

Example: Sal makes out a will leaving certain family heirlooms to her brother Tim, and

80

the rest of her estate to her friend Justine. If Tim fails to survive Sal by 45 days, and no alternate has been named, the heirlooms will go to Justine as Sal's residuary beneficiary. If, however, Sal has named an alternate, then the heirlooms would go to that beneficiary. They would not automatically go to Tim's children. If Sal wants Tim's children to receive the heirlooms in the event Tim fails to survive her, they must be named as alternates.

3. Real Estate Bequests to Children (through C option)

If you leave your real estate to your children in equal shares by selecting the C option, and a child fails to survive you by 45 days, that child's share will pass to his or her living children (your grandchildren), if any. If there are none, then the deceased child's share goes to the other surviving children named under the C option. If there are no such surviving children, the deceased child's share will pass to the alternate(s) named by you. If no alternate(s) are named, the property passes to your residuary estate (i.e., to the beneficiary(s) named to receive the rest of your property).

Example: Janie selects the C option to leave her real estate to her two children, Roy and Ellen. Ellen predeceases Janie but leaves two children of her own. These children will receive Ellen's share. If Ellen left no children, her share would pass to Roy. However, if Roy also predeceased Janie, then the real estate would pass either to an alternate (if Janie named one) or to Janie's residuary estate.

Note: If you wish to name your children as the primary beneficiaries of your real estate, and want a predeceased child's share to go to the other remaining children instead of to the grandchildren, don't use the C option. Instead, if you type in the names of your children in the space provided, WillWriter will distribute the property in the manner described in example 4 just below, in the event one or more of the children fail to survive you by 45 days.

4. Real Estate Bequests To Beneficiaries Typed In By You

If a beneficiary who you have typed in to receive your real estate (i.e., not selected through the C option) fails to survive you by 45 days, that beneficiary's share automatically goes to the remaining surviving beneficiaries named by you to receive your real estate. If there are no such surviving beneficiaries, the real estate passes to the alternate beneficiary(s) named by you. If you failed to name any, the property goes to the residuary estate.

Example: Sal leaves her real estate to her brother Tim and her friend Justine by typing in their names. If Tim fails to survive Sal by 45 days, his share goes to Justine even though Tim leaves children. If Justine also fails to survive Sal by 45 days, then the property will go to the alternate beneficiary(s). If no alternate(s) has been named, the property goes to Sal's residuary estate.

5. Selecting spouse through S option.

If you choose your spouse to inherit your real estate by using the S option, and he or she fails to survive you by 45 days, the property passes either to an alternate you name or to the residuary estate if no alternate has been named.

6. Residuary Bequests (S option, C option and typed in).

Residuary bequests (bequests of the "rest of your property") are handled the same way as the real estate bequests just described with one important exception. If you fail to name an alternate, and there is no surviving named beneficiary (or children of such beneficiary) to take the bequest, your residuary estate may end up passing by intestate succession. So, make sure and name one or more alternates for your residuary estate.

WARNING: If you have found this material a dense lump of lead, remember that you need not be overly concerned with it if you keep your will up-to-date. See Part 12.

D. Adopted and Illegitimate Children

For centuries, courts have been confronted with the issue of whether a gift to "my children" includes adopted children and/or children born out of wedlock. In general, judges will attempt to determine what was intended by the person making the will. Unfortunately, this is often not clear. Most states automatically consider persons adopted while they were minors as "children" for the purpose of a gift to "children." This means that if you have legally adopted a child and leave a gift to "my children" in your will, the adopted child will take his or her share. When using WillWriter, you are asked to name your children. Make sure you name your adopted child, and there will be no problem.

The rule in respect to children born out of wedlock, however, cannot be so clearly stated. This is also true of the situation where a "child" has been adopted after he or she is already an adult. Basically, states recognize an out-of-wedlock child as a "child" of his or her mother unless the child was formally released for adoption. However, an out-of-wedlock child is not a "child" of the father unless the father has legally acknowledged the child as his. Just what constitutes legal acknowledgement differs from state to state.*

Fortunately, if you are the parent of a child born out of wedlock, WillWriter allows you to make sure such child receives exactly what you desire, no more and no less. When WillWriter asks you to name each of your children, name them all, whether they were born when you were married to your current spouse, a previous

---

* This is discussed in detail in Warner & Ihara, The Living Together Kit (Nolo Press). Generally speaking, if a father signs a paternity statement, or later marries the mother, the child is acknowledged for purposes of inheritance and enjoys the same legal standing as a child born to parents who are married.

spouse, or no spouse at all. Then, leave them what you wish. As discussed above, to solve the problem of an "overlooked" child automatically inheriting more than you wished, WillWriter has you leave every child you name $1.00. If this is all you want to give a particular child, fine. You have fulfilled all the legal requirements necessary to avoid the "pretermitted heir" problem discussed in Section B, above. If you wish to give any child more than the $1.00 amount, simply follow WillWriter's instructions.

CLASS GIFT TO CHILDREN NOTE: Under WillWriter, you are asked to leave your residuary estate (all of your property that has not been left to a specific beneficiary under your will) to your spouse, or to your children as a group or class, or to someone else entirely. This can be a very handy thing to do after you have made a number of specific bequests and want to take care of everything that's left over as one bundle. However, some of you may wish to give all the rest of your property to most, but not all, of your children. In other words, you will wish to exclude one or more of your children from this group bequest of the rest of your property. WillWriter gives you a chance to do this by asking you to specify each child you wish to leave out of the class bequest. Then, when your will is printed out, any such child will not appear in the group to receive the property.

E. Bequests to Minors Other Than Your Children

Earlier in this part, we told you that you could appoint a guardian of the estate to care for your childrens' property. However, suppose you wish to leave property to a minor who is not your child. Because minors are presumed to be unable to wisely manage their own property, all states provide that such property be managed by a guardian or custodian until the child reaches majority (in most states, this is 18). Most states have passed a law known as the Uniform Gifts to Minors Act to regulate the procedure by which most personal property can be transferred to a minor through his or her parent or guardian. In addition, a number of states are now passing the Uniform Transfers to Minors Act, an updated version that governs the transfer of all types of property, real and personal.

WillWriter uses these Acts when your will passes property to anyone who is a minor but not your own child. Your will directs your executor to deliver the property to the minor's guardian, who will be the custodian of the property while the child is a minor. In this way, there will be no question as to who the custodian of the property is and what their duties are (these are also spelled out by the Acts).

EXAMPLE: John, an elderly widower, wishes to give the bulk of his estate to his favorite niece, Sally. He makes out his will with Will-Writer and dies while Sally is still a minor. John's executor will deliver her inheritance to Sally's guardians (her parents) to administer for her benefit until she is no longer a minor.

PART 8

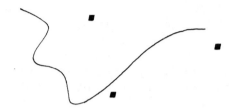

If There Is a Problem
With Your Will

Here we discuss a problem which we think you should be aware of. What happens if there is a discrepancy between what your will provides and the amount or type of property actually left in your probate estate when you die? Put somewhat differently, what happens when you leave people more or different property than is available for distribution at your death?

It can happen that the property people own when they make out their will is not the same as they have when they die. This is especially true if considerable time has passed between these events. Some of the property may have been sold to pay for medical bills. Other items may have been given away. New property may have been acquired, investments changed, real property sold, etc. Further, debts, funeral expenses, probate fees, and, in larger estates, taxes, must be paid before other gifts are distributed.

Obviously, this can raise a number of questions. Where does the money for taxes and debts come from if provision is not made? Also, what happens to all your will provisions if, despite your planning, your spouse "takes against the will" or a child qualifies as being overlooked (a pretermitted heir) and takes a statutory share? Finally, what occurs if property you leave in your will is no longer owned by you when you die? Well, if the specific piece of property (say a particular Tiffany lamp) no longer exists, then the person named in the will to receive it is out of luck. Lawyers call this "ademption." People who don't inherit the property in question are often heard to use an earthier term.

Another similar problem occurs when there isn't enough money to go around. In other words, your will disposes of more than you have. This necessitates what in law is called an "abatement." For example, if you leave $50,000 each to your wife and two kids, but there is only $100,000 in your estate, what happens? Absent a specific directive by the testator (that's you) in the will, the law of each state provides the rules for how the executor of an estate must conduct abatement proceedings. These normally require a pro-rata reduction of bequests if possible without the sale of property. If property must be sold, unspecified property (e.g., "the rest of my property") is generally the first to go, then specific gifts of personal property, then specific gifts of real estate.

Each state's laws differ somewhat on how abatement is to be carried out. WillWriter accedes to such laws, with one exception. If any of your property needs to be sold for abatement purposes, the executor is instructed to dispose of personal property in your "residuary" estate first. Your residuary estate is all of your property which has not been specifically described and left to someone by your will. Thus, if you leave "the rest of your property" to your children, this property would be considered the residuary estate and disposed of first for abatement purposes. Put another way, if there is a shortage, the people who receive the "rest of your property" will lose out to those to whom you made specific bequests (e.g., my car, my house, my cat, $10,000). If the residuary estate is still not sufficient to account for a deficit in your probate estate, the executor is directed to abate in the most equitable (fair) way possible consistent with state law.

EXAMPLE: Freida, a widow, makes a will which contains the following bequests:

• My house to my sister Hillary;

• My coin collection (appraised at $30,000) to my three children;

• My three antique chandeliers to my brother Herbert;

• The rest of my property to my companion Denise. [Although not spelled out in the will, this consists of a savings account ($6,000), a car ($5,000), a camera ($1,000) and $5000 worth of stock.]

When Freida dies, it turns out she owes $25,000 worth of debts, which she has made no provision to pay. The probate fees amount to an additional $5,000. What would happen if Freida had used WillWriter? To meet the estate's liability of $30,000, the executor would first turn to the residuary estate. Since this has a total value of $17,000--$13,000 short of the $30,000 goal--the entire residuary estate will have to be sold. This means that Denise will get nothing under the will. Further, since the residuary estate did not cover the estate's total indebtedness, the executor will now have to choose whether to sell the house, the coin collection and /or the chandeliers. Exactly how this decision is made will depend on the laws of the states where Freida died and where the house is situated.

WARNING: The subject of what happens if you leave more property in your will than is actually available is far too complex to cover here in any meaningful detail. However, the overall point is relatively simple. Don't give away more than you own, after what you owe and what your estate will need to pay in tax is subtracted. Make a new will whenever your property situation changes significantly. If you are concerned about how your property will be distributed in the event an abatement (reduction of gifts) is required (i.e., your estate comes up short), consult an attorney knowledgeable in such matters.

PART 9

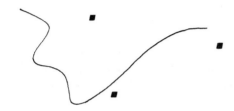

Sample Uses of WillWriter

In our introduction in Part 1, we presented
an overview of the different options available
to the user of the WillWriter program. Then,
throughout the middle portions of this manual,
we reviewed the ways you can use WillWriter to
deal with the common types of issues involved
with wills and estate planning. Now, let's be
more specific as to the type of will you can
prepare using WillWriter.

The WillWriter program allows you to write a
will that is simple, accurate and legal. Further, whenever circumstances change you can use
WillWriter to make appropriate changes and thus
keep your will completely up-to-date, without
the inconvenience and expense of a lawyer.
WillWriter is completely appropriate for single
persons, unmarried couples and single parents,
as well as for married couples. Of course, as
we mentioned in the introduction, WillWriter

does not allow you every conceivable option as to the disposition of your property. However, the choices WillWriter does offer provide far more flexibility than the "Check the Boxes" wills introduced in some states, and should be adequate for the needs of most low- and middle-income Americans.

A. What WillWriter Can Do

Let's look at some of the things you can accomplish by using WillWriter:

● You can use Willwriter to leave all of your real and personal property to your spouse.

EXAMPLE: Laurence and Betty are married and have three children. Laurence owns one-half of their family home, a car, a boat left to him by his father, some antique coins and a personal computer. Laurence and Betty have agreed that each should leave the other all his or her property and that the survivor will then leave all of the property in equal shares to the children. Accordingly, Laurence uses WillWriter to leave all of his personal property and all of his real estate interest to Betty, as his spouse.

● If you are not married, but live with someone, WillWriter allows you to leave all your real and personal property to that person.

EXAMPLE 1: Assume that everything is the same as with the previous example, except that Laurence and Betty are not married. This time Laurence leaves all of his personal property and all of his real property to Betty as an individual. If Laurence were still married to someone else, but living with Betty, he might run into family protection problems in many states. See Part 5, Sections C and D.

EXAMPLE 2: Darryl and Floyd have lived together for several years. Darryl wants to leave Floyd all of his possessions in the event he

should die. He can use WillWriter to accomplish
this.

• In either of the above situations, you can
use WillWriter to leave a portion of your property to your spouse (or person you live with)
and make specific gifts of personal property
items or cash to your children, relatives,
friends or charities.

EXAMPLE: Laurence leaves his interest in the
family home to his spouse, Betty, his coin collection to one of his children, his boat to
another child, his computer to a charity assisting the deaf, and $500 to his Aunt Agnes.

• If you are single or divorced, WillWriter
allows you to leave your property as you see
fit, except that you cannot split your real
estate.

EXAMPLE: Leonard, a lifelong bachelor, completely disposes of all his personal possessions
by describing specific items to be left to particular relatives and friends. He leaves his
house to his favorite charity.

• You can use WillWriter to leave all your

real and personal property to your children, or a charitable institution, or any other persons of your choice.*

EXAMPLE 1: Laurence places his interest in the family home in joint tenancy with Betty and leaves all the rest of his property to his children in equal shares.

EXAMPLE 2: Although Morton is now married to Becky and has three children from previous marriages, he decides he wants to leave his land, his cars, and his expensive stereo equipment to his best friend, Jim. WillWriter permits him to do this, but if Morton lives in a state following the common law property system, Becky may have a right to a share of this property by operation of law. See Part 5, Sections C and D.

• You can use WillWriter to leave a large number of personal property bequests (e.g., heirlooms, cash, motor vehicles, tools, furniture) to up to sixteen separate people or institutions.

EXAMPLE 1: Annie and Bill Webber have three children--Ellen, Lance and Chuck. Annie could leave her jewelry, bird and clothes to Ellen, her collection of first editions to Bill, a cash bequest of $5,000 to Lance, her vintage 1950 Mercury Stationwagon to Chuck, a bequest of $500 to the Third World Refugee Committee, and so on.

• You can use WillWriter to designate alternate recipients of your gifts in the event the

---

* But remember, as we discussed in Part 5, it is not wise to try and completely disinherit your spouse if you live in a common law property state unless your spouse has been previously well provided for outside of the will and agrees with your estate plan (see Part 5, Sections C and D).

primary recipients do not survive you by at least 45 days.* If you do not do this, the property passes into your residuary estate in the event the primary recipient fails to survive you. This means it goes to whoever you have named to receive "the rest of your property."

EXAMPLE: Annie, of the previous example, designates Chuck as the alternative recipient of the first editions in the event Bill does not survive her by 45 days. If she had named no alternative, and Bill failed to survive her by 45 days, the gift to Bill would pass into Annie's residuary estate (i.e., "the rest of my personal property").

• You can use WillWriter to designate your spouse, some or all of your children, or specific individuals (including a child) and institutions to inherit all of your remaining property (whatever is left after you have made one or more specific bequests of personal property and real estate). If more than one beneficiary is designated, each will take an equal share.

EXAMPLE: Annie could make the specific gifts mentioned above and then leave the rest of her property to Bill (or any other person or institution of her choice).

WARNING: It is very important that you name a beneficiary to receive your residuary estate (the rest of your property not specifically disposed of). Otherwise, any property that you have not specifically left to someone, and any property left to non-surviving beneficiaries (where alternates have not been named or do not survive either) will be distributed according to the intestate laws of your state.

• You can use WillWriter to designate your spouse, some or all of your children, or specific individuals (including a child) and institutions to inherit all of your real estate. If

---

* This 45-day period is a recognition of the delays caused by probate or the administration of the estate. If the first-named recipient of your gift(s) is not alive at the end of this period, the alternate will be entitled to them.

more than one beneficiary is designated, all
will take equal shares. Before you leave real
estate in your will, however, you should be
thoroughly familiar with the routine probate
avoidance techniques we discuss in Part 6*.

EXAMPLE 1: Doug, a 60-year-old unmarried
man, has lived with Brenda for 25 years. In
addition to various items of personal property,
he owns a house and a ski cabin. Doug transfers
the house and cabin into a living trust, with
Brenda as the beneficiary.

EXAMPLE 2: Assume now that Doug is a 45-
year-old real estate speculator who owns eight
different parcels of real estate. Because he
doesn't expect to hold on to this property until
he dies, Doug will find it easier to leave his
real estate to Brenda in his will, despite the
possibility of large probate fees should he die
prematurely. This way, property can be sold and
new property purchased without the need to do
and undo trusts or joint tenancy arrangements.
Later, when Doug is older, he can create a
sophisticated estate plan so that his real property avoids probate.

EXAMPLE 3: Now assume that Doug is 65 years
old, but that now he is married to Brenda, and
the father of three children. His sole real
estate ownership consists of the family house

---

* These are especially useful when your property is not
likely to change much before you die and you know who you
want to receive it. On the other hand, if you are in good
health and anticipate a number of changes in respect to your
real estate or your desires before you die, you may wish to
use WillWriter to dispose of the real estate (despite the
possibility of high probate fees). This is because it is
easy to use WillWriter to update your will as the situation
changes and circumstances dictate, and somewhat more difficult to use such probate avoidance devices as a joint tenancy or life insurance. Put differently, when you use probate
avoidance techniques, you may have to do and undo some red
tape every time you buy and sell property or decide to
change beneficiaries. For this reason, younger people in
good health might reasonably decide to bypass probate avoidance techniques in favor of a will, at least until a more
sophisticated estate plan appears appropriate.

which he inherited from his parents. Here, Doug might wish to place the house in joint tenancy with, or in a living trust for, Brenda and use WillWriter to dispose of personal property items of lesser value.

● You can name a personal guardian for your children in the event there is no surviving natural or adoptive parent able to care for them. The probate court has the right to review your choice, but will probably accept it unless the person refuses to take on the responsibility, or someone comes forward with evidence that the best interests of your children would be better served by their being in someone else's custody. See Part 7(A).

● WillWriter gives you the option of naming a separate person or institution (e.g., a bank, if its rules permit it to accept the responsibility) as a financial guardian to manage the property you are leaving your children. Or, you can name the same person to serve as both personal guardian and guardian of the estate. See Part 7(A).

● You can name an executor for your estate. The executor is responsible for making sure the provisions in your will are properly carried out. This can be any competent person over eighteen years of age and is commonly either a spouse, a close knowledgeable relative or a financial institution (bank, savings and loan, etc.). Many institutions have specific internal guidelines determining the kinds and sizes of estates of which they will and will not serve as executors. Also, some individuals would find it a great hardship to serve in this capacity. Accordingly, before you select an executor, you should check with the person or institution to make sure s/he or it will assume the responsibility.

EXAMPLE 1: Bill and Annie don't wish to burden their relatives with having to take care of their fairly considerable estate, and each accordingly names the Third National Bank as their executor after checking that this bank will, in fact, be willing to serve as an executor for their estates.

EXAMPLE 2: Bill and Annie both execute wills naming each other as executors in case the other dies first. In the event they both die simultaneously, Bill and Annie name Annie's father as an alternate executor, after obtaining his permission.

B. What WillWriter Cannot Do

Now let's look at what WillWriter cannot do:

● You cannot use WillWriter to leave conditional bequests, except to provide that if the first person named to get the property fails to survive you by 45 days, the property goes to a second named beneficiary.

EXAMPLE: Let's assume you wish to leave your dog to Aunt Millie if Aunt Millie continues living in your town (or graduates from a school of veterinary medicine), but to your sister Kate in the event Millie has moved away at the time of your death (or becomes an orthodontist instead of a veterinarian). WillWriter does not let you accomplish this. However, if you wish to leave your dog to Millie if she survives you by 45 days, otherwise to your sister Kate, WillWriter will work just fine. If you fail to name Kate as an alternative, or Kate also dies within the 45 days, your dog would become part of your residuary estate and go to whoever gets the rest of your property.

• You cannot use Willwriter to make bequests that take effect in some future period of time, i.e., all bequests become effective when you die.

EXAMPLE: Emory wants his grandchildren to inherit his house, but also wants his sister to live in the house until her death. To do this, Emory would have to leave his house to his sister for her life (this is called a "life estate") and then to his grandchildren upon his sister's death. Because the bequest to the grandchildren would take effect in the future, Emory could not use WillWriter to accomplish his desire. However, he could use WillWriter for his other property and use a trust to dispose of his house as he wishes.

• You cannot use Willwriter to split your real estate.

EXAMPLE: You own several pieces of real estate (say, a home, a hunting cabin and a piece of undeveloped property) and want to leave each parcel to a different person. WillWriter won't let you accomplish this. If you are willing to leave all of your real estate to one person, or equally to your children, or other beneficiaries, WillWriter is quite adequate for your needs.

One reason we have not designed WillWriter to handle bequests of multiple pieces of real property to different people is because we believe many people will choose to use one or more of the probate avoidance techniques to pass most or all of their real property without use of a will. However, as we mentioned above, this may not be the case for younger people whose real estate ownership situation is fluid and who are uncertain about who should ultimately end up with the property. If such people own a lot of real property and desire to split it among two or more persons (unless they leave it to two or more beneficiaries in equal shares), they should see a lawyer.

• You cannot use Willwriter to create a testamentary trust in your will.* As we've seen, trusts are legal devices by which property can be left in the care of one person (called the "trustee") for the use of another person (called a "beneficiary"). When they are used in wills to control the ways property left to beneficiaries will be handled, they are called "testamentary trusts." Most people do not need this type of trust. They are useful, however, if you have a large estate which you wish to leave to minor children or incompetent adults. Other types of testamentary trusts are valuable to do tax planning in larger estates. We mention this use of trusts briefly in Part 6(C). Most trusts must be individually crafted to be useful, and therefore aren't appropriate for WillWriter.

EXAMPLE: Zeke wants to leave his nineteen-

---

* A testamentary trust passes ownership of the property placed in the trust to the beneficiary at death. Control of the property is given to the trustee for the benefit of the beneficiary. This is not the same as either a revocable living (intervivos) trust or a revocable "Totten" (savings bank) trust under which you can set up a trust during your life and appoint yourself trustee of your own property, with the property to go to the beneficiary outright at your death. Living (intervivos) trusts, which are primarily valuable to avoid probate, are discussed in more detail in Part 6(B) of this manual.

98

year-old child, Rainbow, $500,000, but doubts that Rainbow has the experience to spend the money wisely. Accordingly, he wants to create a trust under which a trustee will spend the money for Rainbow's needs until she turns 25. This cannot be done by using WillWriter. However, if Rainbow were under 18, WillWriter would allow Zeke to achieve a somewhat similar result by naming a separate guardian of the estate to handle Rainbow's money until she turns 18.

● You cannot use WillWriter to require your guardian or executor to purchase a bond. A bond is a legally binding guarantee by a bonding company (usually an insurance company) that the person bonded will not wrongfully dispose of funds with which he or she is entrusted. Because the premium or fee which must be paid for a bond usually comes out of the estate, with the result that there is less money for the beneficiaries, most wills which involve the disposition of small or moderate estates do not require one. Instead, care is taken to appoint persons who are known to be trustworthy. Following this general practice, WillWriter does not provide for a bond. However, we do encourage you to appoint trustworthy people.

● You cannot use Willwriter to establish a plan to dispose of your remains. Wills are simply not the best way to explain what you want done with your remains after you die. Why? Because wills are normally located and read long after the fact. It is accordingly wise to leave specific instructions to those who will take responsibility for your funeral arrangements. It is also wise to both arrange and pay for funeral and burial (or cremation) details in advance.

PART 10

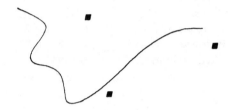

Checklist for Making Out Your Will

We've covered a lot of ground in this manual. Here now is a checklist of the concrete steps you must take to prepare a valid and effective will.

STEP 1. Determine what is in your net estate. If you have not already done so, fill out the form contained in Part 5. If you are married, make sure you know what property is yours and what belongs to your spouse. Rules vary, depending on the state of your residence and the location of your real property. See Part 5(B).

STEP 2. Figure out how much of this property is appropriate to be transferred free of probate by carefully reading Part 6(B) and, if you need or desire additional information, Plan Your Estate by Denis Clifford.

STEP 3. For larger estates, figure out how much of your property ownership can sensibly be transferred during your life, thereby saving on estate taxes (see Part 6, Section C). If your estate is very large, see a lawyer and/or accountant specializing in estate tax planning and read Plan Your Estate.

STEP 4. Use Willwriter to list all your children, whether natural, adopted, or out of wedlock, and the children of any child who has died. As explained in Part 7, WillWriter will automatically leave these children (or grandchildren) $1.00 in addition to whatever other property you leave them, to assure that they are not considered as overlooked or "pretermitted" heirs. Again, if you plan to leave any of these children property, they will receive such property plus $1.00 more.

STEP 5. Use WillWriter to designate which specific items of property or cash should go to which people under your will.

STEP 6. Use Willwriter to designate who is to receive your real estate if not subjected to probate avoidance techniques.

STEP 7. Use Willwriter to designate who is to receive the rest of your property not otherwise specified or subjected to probate avoidance techniques.

STEP 8. If you reside in a common law state, read Part 5(C) of this manual to make sure your spouse is receiving at least his or her minimum statutory share of your estate.

STEP 9. If you are using WillWriter to leave a great deal of property to a charitable institution, check to see if the laws of your state restrict your right to make this gift (see Part 5, Section F).

STEP 10. Make sure your anticipated estate which is left after you take advantage of probate avoidance techniques, and which is therefore eligible to be left in your will, roughly

CHOCOLATE COVERED
CHERRIES - MY FAVORITE.

matches the property you dispose of in your
will.

STEP 11. If you have minor children, use
WillWriter to select a person and an alternate
to serve as personal guardian in the event no
natural or adoptive parent is able or willing to
care for your children after you die. If you
desire your minor childrens' property to be
handled by someone other than their personal
guardian, you should use WillWriter to specify a
separate guardian for such property.

STEP 12. You should nominate an executor to
handle your estate.

STEP 13. Finally, depending on the degree of
your uncertainty and/or confusion about any of
these matters, and the amount of property you
have (the value of your estate), you may want to
have your will checked by an attorney in your
state.

PART 11

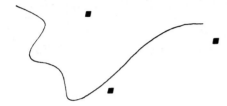

Formalities

A. Signing and Witnessing Your Will

A will must be properly executed to be valid.
This means that you must sign your will in front
of witnesses. And, these witnesses must not
only sign the will in your presence, but also in
the presence of the other witnesses.

While state laws vary as to how many witnesses you need, three meets the requirements of
every state. Even if your state only requires
two witnesses, three is better because it provides one more person to establish that your
signature is valid during probate.

There are few requirements for witnesses--
they need only be:

• Over 18 and of sound mind;

• People who will not inherit under the will.
That means anyone who is a recipient of any gift
should not be a witness;

• Finally, if possible, the people should be
easy to locate in the event of your death. This
usually means choosing people who don't move
around a lot and who are younger than you are.

See Part 12 on updating your will.

IMPORTANT NOTE: In over half the states, a will can usually be probated without your witnesses being available after your death. In 23 states, however, your executor may need to locate and produce in court one or more of your witnesses after your death, unless you and your witnesses sign your will in front of a notary public. These states are: Arkansas, Connecticut, Delaware, Florida, Indiana, Iowa, Kansas, Kentucky, Massachusetts, Missouri, New Hampshire, New Jersey, North Carolina, Oklahoma, Oregon, Pennsylvania, Rhode Island, Tennessee, Texas, Virginia, Washington, West Virginia, and Wyoming.

While it may be inconvenient for you and your witnesses to all visit a notary public at the same time, and although your will is perfectly valid without notarization, WillWriter does provide a "notarization" option (called a "self-proving will"), for those of you who wish to make the probate process as simple as possible. This is especially recommended for residents of the states listed above. Remember, though, notarization only makes sense if your will leaves enough assets to make formal probate likely. Also, you must have your signature witnessed as described in Chapter 11, even though you choose the notarization option. If, after reading Part 6 of the manual, you conclude that your will will not be probated, there is no point in getting it notarized in any state. See Chapter 13.

Here is how to go about arranging for the witnessing of your will, whether or not a notary is present:

• Have the three witnesses assemble in one place;

• Tell them that the papers you hold constitute your last will and testament. They don't need to know what is in it;

• Have them watch you sign your will;

• Remember to sign the will using exactly the

same form of spelling of your name as you provide in the WillWriter program. This should be the way you sign such formal documents as deeds, checks and loan applications;

• Have the witnesses sign in the appropriate place on your will while all of you watch. The clause immediately preceding the witnesses' signature states ("attests") that the above events have in fact occurred.

IMPORTANT: As mentioned, there is no requirement that the witnesses read your will or that you read it to them. However, they must realize that you intend the document to be your "last will and testament." A little ritual dialogue can be helpful here:

You: "This is my will;"

Witnesses: "He says it is his will;"

You: "I am of sound mind;"

Witnesses: "He seems to be of sound mind."

While this may seem somewhat strained or sound a bit like a Gilbert and Sullivan routine, it may help get the group into a good mood for celebrating the fact that you just accomplished an important task. And you did it yourself.

B. Don't Alter Your Will

Once you have produced a printed will by using WillWriter, it is extremely important that you not alter it by inserting handwritten or typed additions or changes. Do not do this, either before or after you sign it. Do not even correct mispellings. The laws of most states require that any additions or changes in a will, even clerical ones, be done in a formal way. This involves making a new will, or a codicil (formal addition) to the existing one. One of the great advantages of WillWriter is that you can conveniently update or change your will by simply putting the WillWriter floppy disk into your computer and making a new will. So, you have no excuse for attempting possibly illegal shortcuts. See Part 12 below.

C. Copying and Storing Your Will

Once your will is properly signed, what do you do with it next? Your main consideration should be that upon your death the right people know that your will exists and where it is located. Accordingly, it is often a good idea to make one or two unsigned copies (or "will summaries"). Give one to your proposed executor and, if it is appropriate, another to your spouse or children. Your original properly-executed will should be in a safe-deposit box or other safe place, such as a metal fire proof box in your home.*

What do you do with the WillWriter disk? After all, once you've printed out your will, you still have a copy of it in electronic form. Our suggestion is that you find a safe private place to store it so that you can use it to update your will if that becomes necessary, and at the same time others will not have access to it without your permission. If you have a safe deposit box, store it there along with your will.

NOTE: As with other unsigned and unwitnessed copies, the copy of your will stored on the WillWriter disk does not constitute a valid will until it is printed out and formally "executed" (signed and witnessed), as indicated earlier in this chapter.

---

* Despite good intentions, it is often hard to find a will at death, and even harder to find other types of personal property such as bank books and insurance policies. One good way to save your loved ones the misery of searching for important papers when they are already dealing with the grief of losing you is to make a clear record of all your property, its location and the location of any ownership documents that relate to it, including your will. Your Family Records: How to Preserve Personal, Financial and Legal History by Pladsen & Clifford (Nolo Press) offers an excellent way to do this. Some people are tempted to prepare more than one signed and executed original of their will in case one is lost. While in most states the preparation and execution of duplicate originals (each one must be separately signed and witnessed--you can't just prepare one and photocopy it) is legal, we do not normally recommend it. This is because if you later want to change your will, it can be difficult to locate all the old ones to destroy them.

PART 12

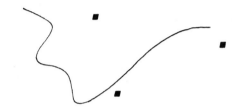

Updating Your Will

A. When Should You Change Your Will

By now it should be clear to you that what your will contains is heavily dependent on the circumstances. The state of your residence, your marital status, the extent of your estate, whether you have children, and whether a child predeceases you, leaving children of his or her own are all examples of variables which greatly determine how your will operates after your death. As these or other variables change between the time you make your will and the day you die, you will want to update your will to reflect such changes. One of the great advantages of WillWriter is that it permits you to easily change your will without having to visit a lawyer and pay a fee each time you do. Such visits are usually necessary with a lawyer-drawn will, since alterations to a will (codicils) must be drafted and signed with the same formal-ity as the original. With WillWriter, however, you can just make a new will that incorporates the changes. As we describe in Section B below, this is amazingly simple to do.

Here are the situations where you will definitely want to update your will (by making a new one with WillWriter):

● If you change your mind about who you want to have your property;

● If you move to a different state (especially from a community property state to a common law state, or vice versa).

As we indicated earlier, the law which is used to interpret wills is generally as follows:

1. For personal property, the law of the state where the testator (or person making the will) is domiciled (living) at the time of death, and

2. In respect to the disposition of real estate, the law of the state where it is located.

WillWriter is tailored to help you make a valid will according to the state you list as your state of residence. Thus, WillWriter presents you with different choices, depending on whether you live in a community property state or a common law property state. Because of this, the will you made in your old state may be defective in your new one.

● If your marital status changes.

Suppose that after you use WillWriter to leave all or part of your property to your spouse, the two of you get divorced. What happens? As with so many other questions, the answer will differ depending on your state. In many states, the divorce automatically cancels the bequest to the ex-spouse, and, if you have made no residuary bequest in your will (i.e., leaving the rest of your property to someone), your remaining heirs would take by intestate succession. In other states, however, your ex-spouse would still inherit as per the will. If there is a remarriage, the issue becomes even more murky. For this reason, we strongly recommend that you not include your spouse in your will if a divorce is pending or imminent. Also, if you later get divorced after making out a will, it would be wise to make a brand new will and destroy the old one, as we suggested in Part 10.

- If you have or adopt new children.

Each time a child is born or legally adopted into your family, it is wise to review your will. The new child should be named in the will and provided for according to your wishes.

- If any of your children die before you, leaving children of their own.

If a child dies before you do, and leaves children of his or her own, these children (your grandchildren) may receive an automatic share of your estate (in most states) unless you either provide for them in some way, or they receive property that was left to the deceased child, or you indicate in the will that you desire not to provide for them. In Part 7, Sections C and D, we explain how WillWriter handles this situation. To make sure that your will effectively carries out your intentions, you should check and alter it accordingly if one of your children dies before you.

- If any of your primary beneficiaries die and you have not named an alternate or wish to name someone else.

If a primary beneficiary you have named to receive either a significant specific bequest or the "rest of your property" dies before you, you should update your will if you desire a new primary beneficiary to be named. This would especially be important if you failed to name an alternate, or the alternate you named is no longer your first choice as the beneficiary for the particular bequest.

If the property in your estate changes materially.

• If your probate estate (the property you leave in your will) either expands or shrinks between the time you make your will and the time you die, you should review your will to make sure it realistically reflects your current situation. This is especially true if there are changes in your ownership of real estate or expensive personal property items. Otherwise, you may be faced with the problems discussed in Part 8.

• If the person(s) you named as guardian for your children are no longer available to serve.

The person(s) named to serve as a guardian for your minor children may move away, become disabled, or simply turn out to be not the kind of person you would have care for your children. If so, you will want to make a new will naming somebody else who will be more suitable.

UPDATING YOUR FILE

• If the person(s) or institution named as executor is no longer able to serve.

The executor of your estate is the person charged with making sure your wishes are faithfully complied with. You may find out that the person or institution you originally named would really not be the best person for this task. If so, you should write a new will and change executors.

• If your witnesses move away or otherwise become unavailable to testify in the event a dispute over the validity of your signature arises, or it is otherwise necessary to prove your will.

B. How to Change Your Will with WillWriter

The first step in changing your will with WillWriter should be to get your old disk out of its storage place and boot it. Since you have a will stored on it, the program will automatically go right to a "menu" screen that provides you with several options. One of these is "R." Type "R" and "Return." You will then be presented with a screen showing the various items that you can review and change if desired. Each item has a number next to it. By typing the appropriate number and pressing "Return," you will be taken to the relevant screen, your prior response will be displayed, and you will be asked whether you wish to change it.

For most of the items you will be reviewing, you will be given an opportunity to make the desired changes and then, by pressing return, to return directly to the review screen. For some items, however, you will be told that a change will require you to continue through the rest of the program rather than returning directly to the review screen. That is because certain items, such as your marital status, your state, and whether you have children, determine the information presented and the questions asked by WillWriter. If you choose, you may then make the appropriate change. If you choose not to make a change, you will be returned to the review screen. This process is spelled out in more detail in the User's Manual (see Part 14).

C. What to Do with Your Altered Will

Your altered will is, in fact, a brand new will and must be signed and witnessed just as your first one was. This includes notarization if you are in one of the 23 states where this is advisable and you choose to do so. Generally, it cancels or revokes all prior wills which are inconsistent with it. However, it is extremely important that you not rely on this automatic cancellation. If you allow two different wills to exist at the same time, you court the possibility that your intentions will not be carried out. So, once you've made your new will, make sure the original (and, if possible, all existing copies) of your former will is retrieved and destroyed.

PART 13

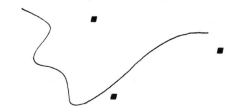

Understanding Your Will's Language

In our introduction in Part 1, we stressed that wills are made up of magic phrases that can be relied on to give full effect to the testator's intent. The will produced by WillWriter is no different, although we have simplified some language where it is safe to do so.

Because many of you will read your will and want to understand what it says, we provide here an annotation for each important clause that we feel could stand some explaining.

● "I revoke all wills and codicils that I have previously made."

COMMENT: In the event you leave more than one will in existence, this clause tells the court you only intended your latest will to be valid.

● "I am married to _____."

COMMENT: This clause establishes the person you are married to when you make the will as the person who will inherit as your spouse under your will when you die. If your marital status changes, it is accordingly necessary to change this portion of the will. See Part 12.

● "I have ___ children now living, whose names are:"

COMMENT: By simply listing all your children here, whether natural, adopted, or out of wedlock, you will prevent them from being considered as "overlooked" (pretermitted) in most states. See Part 7(B).

● "However, if this person or entity does not survive me by 45 days, I revoke the above bequest or devise which shall instead be made to:"

COMMENT: Since property is generally not distributed as part of probate until sometime after the testator's death, this provision provides an alternative recipient for your property in the event your first choice does not survive the 45-day period. Some wills make this period longer (180 days is common), to conform more closely with the time it takes to complete probate and actually turn property over to a beneficiary. WillWriter uses a 45-day period because small estates will often be exempt from probate, and the formalities necessary to actually transfer property can often be completed within this time period.

● If any beneficiary, other than my child (or children), of any specific personal property bequest made by this will, fails to survive me by 45 days, and no alternative beneficiary has been named in this will to receive the bequest, such bequest shall pass into my residuary estate.

COMMENT: Under this clause, if a specific bequest of personal property is made to a designated beneficiary who is not one of your named children, and who fails to survive you by 45 days, and you have not named an alternate bene-

ficiary, your bequest will pass into your residuary estate. This clause does not apply to
residuary bequests or bequests (devises) of real
estate. Those situations are covered later in
this chapter.

● "If any of my children fail to survive me by
45 days, specific personal property bequests
made to them by this will, for which an alternative beneficiary has not been named, shall be
given to the deceased child's living children in
equal shares. In the event no alternative beneficiary has been named in this will to receive
the bequest, and my deceased child has left no
children of his or her own, such bequest shall
pass into my residuary estate."

COMMENT: In the event your will leaves property to a child who doesn't survive you, the
laws of most states provide that the property
will pass directly to the grandchildren. This
technical legal provision provides that any
property left to that child will be evenly divided among such grandchildren. This provision
would only become operative if you: 1) fail to
make a new will in the event one of your children dies before you, 2) you left property to
that child, and 3) you failed to name an alternate recipient for that property in the event
your child predeceased you. This provision does
not apply when your childred are beneficiaries
of your real estate or your residuary estate.
Again, we believe it is much better to simply
make a new will should one of your children die
before you, so that this clause will not prove
necessary.

● "I hereby leave $1.00 to each of the fol-
lowing (list all children and children of deceased children) __ persons: including any
afterborn and adopted child, in addition to and
not in lieu of any other gift, bequest, or
devise to such child, children or grandchildren."

COMMENT: By providing $1.00 to each person
named by you as a child, or child of a predeceased child, you will be telling the court that
you didn't overlook such persons in your will.

Although the language includes all afterborn and adopted children, we strongly urge you to change your will to specifically name any new child, natural or adopted. The language makes clear that you intend the named children (and grandchildren) to receive the $1.00 in addition to any other bequest or devise you may have left them in the will. See Part 7(B) and 7(C) of this manual for more details.

• "I give all of my real property, together with any insurance on that property, and subject to any encumbrances on it at the time of my death, including any mortgage, deed of trust, and real property taxes and assessments, to _____. If any beneficiary named to receive this property fails to survive me by 45 days, his or her share shall pass to the remaining surviving beneficiaries named above to receive my real estate. If there are no such surviving beneficiaries, my real estate shall pass to: (alternate) (residuary)."

Comment: This provision applies to real estate bequests made to beneficiaries whose names are typed in rather than selected through the C option. Under it, if a beneficiary fails to survive you by 45 days, his or her share passes to the remaining benficiaries named to receive the real estate. If there are none, then the real estate passes to the alternate(s), or to your residuary estate if you have named no alternates. This provision only operates if a named beneficiary does not survive you by 45 days, and you have not updated your will. See Part 7 Section C for details.

• "If any child named to receive my real estate fails to survive me by 45 days, that child's living children shall take that child's share in equal shares. If a child named to receive my real estate fails to survive me by 45 days and leaves no children of his or her own, that child's share shall be divided in equal shares among any other surviving children named above to receive my real estate. If there are no such surviving children, the deceased child's share shall pass to: (Alternate) (Residuary)."

116

Comment: This provison applies to real estate bequests made to your children through use
of the C option. If a child named under this
provision fails to survive you by 45 days, his
or her children take that share. If there are no
such grandchildren, the share passes to the
other children named by you. If there are no
such other children, the share goes to the alternate you have named (or to your residuary
estate if you have named no alternate). Again,
this language operates when a named beneficiary
fails to survive you by 45 days and you haven't
updated your will. See Part 7 Section C for
details.

• "I give the residuary estate, i.e. the rest
of my property not otherwise specifically disposed of by this will or in any other manner,
to: _____."

Comment on Residuary Estate Clauses: The
will provisions and accompanying comments just
presented for real estate bequests are essentially the same for bequests made to your residuary
estate. We strongly recommend that you keep your
will up-to-date if you wish to avoid having these
provisions take effect. Also, we recommend that
you name one or more alternates to inherit your
residuary estate. See Part 7 Section C for details.

• "I hereby grant to my executor the following powers, to be exercised as he or she deems
to be in the best interests of my estate: 1) To
retain property without liability for loss or
depreciation resulting from such retention, etc.

Comment: This clause (not fully repeated
here) gives your executor broad discretion to
carry out a number of activities without having
to first seek court approval, in all states that
recognize an executor's independent power. This
generally cuts down the length of time it takes
to get your will through probate. The law of
some states may grant an executor some or all of
these powers without enumeration. However, the
fact that WillWriter expressly sets them out in
your will won't hurt. Although some of these
powers may seem a little broad, we believe they
make good sense as long as you choose an execu-

tor who you have confidence in. After all, your executor has a fiduciary duty (duty of trust) to carry out the provisions of your will.

• "If any beneficiary under this will, in any manner, directly or indirectly, contests or attacks this will or any or its provisions, any share or interest in my estate given to the contesting beneficiary under this will is re-voked and shall be disposed of in the same manner provided herein as if that contesting beneficiary had predeceased me without issue."

COMMENT: This formidable clause attempts to disinherit anyone who tries to invalidate the will or receive more than what the will pro-vides. In some situations, this type of clause is effective. However, you should know that many courts will find ways to allow heirs to both challenge a will and still inherit in the event their challenge fails.

• "If my spouse and I should die simultan-eously, or under such circumstances as to render it difficult or impossible to determine who predeceased the other, I shall be conclusively presumed to have survived my spouse for purposes of this will."

COMMENT: This clause provides an orderly system for determining whose heirs inherit what property in the event you and your spouse die at the same time. Here is the way it works. If you and your spouse suffer a simultaneous death, the court will interpret your will as if your spouse had died before you. Property that you left to your spouse will then pass directly to your other heirs as determined by the intestate laws of your state. The same arrangement will apply to your spouse. This means that each of your estates will pass to your own heirs rather than to each other's heirs. Also, your property will only pass through probate once.

• "If 45 days after my death there is no living person who is both entitled by law to the custody of my minor child or children and avail-able to assume such custody, I recommend that _____ be appointed personal guardian of such minor child or children, to serve without bond."

118

COMMENT: This clause permits you to recommend a personal guardian for all of your children. The language of the clause recognizes that your choice for guardian will only be adopted by the court if the child's other surviving natural or adoptive parent is either not legally qualified to assume custody over the children or not available to do so. The word "recommend" is used because your choice is not binding on the court if the court determines that the best interests of the child require another choice. The guardian will not be required to post a bond for the reasons discussed in Part 9(B).

● "If at my death any of my children are minors, I recommend that _____ be appointed Guardian of the Estate of the minor child or children, to serve without bond."

COMMENT: This clause expresses your desire that the person or institution you name be appointed to care for the property of your minor child or children until they become adults. If such child or children have a surviving natural or adoptive parent who assumes custody, that custody will also usually involve control over the child's or children's property despite your recommendation in this clause. However, if the court appoints a personal guardian, then your recommendation in this clause will be followed in most states if the court finds it to be in the best interests of the child. This guardian of the estate will serve without posting a bond for the reasons stated in Part 9(B).

● "If any person not my child who receives property under this will is a minor at the time of distribution, I direct my executor to distribute the property to the minor's guardian under the provisions of the Uniform Gifts to Minors Act, or the Uniform Transfers to Minors Act, enacted by the state of _____, if either is applicable."

COMMENT: This clause directs your executor to use the Uniform Gifts to Minors Act (or Uniform Transfers to Minors Act) to distribute property to a minor other than your child, assuming that your state allows such act to be used for bequests or devises made by will.

119

● "I nominate _____ as executor of this will, to serve without bond. If _____ shall for any reason fail to qualify or cease to act as executor, I nominate _____ , also to serve without bond."

COMMENT: This provision names the person(s) to serve as the executor of your will. The executor will serve without bond for the reasons discussed in Part 9(B).

● I, _____ , the testator, sign my name to this instrument, consisting of ____pages, including this page signed by me, this _____day of _____, 19__, and do hereby declare that I sign and execute this instrument as my last will and that I sign it willingly, that I execute it as my free and voluntary act for the purposes therein expressed, and that I am of the age of majority or otherwise legally empowered to make a will, and under no contraint or undue influence.

_____

● We, the witnesses, sign our names to this instrument, and do hereby declare that the testator signs and executes this instrument as his last will and that he signs it willingly, and that each of us, in the presence and hearing of the testator, and in the presence of each other, hereby signs this will as witness to the testator's signing, and that to the best of our knowledge the testator is of the age of majority, or is otherwise legally empowered to make a will, and under no contraint or undue influence. We declare, under penalty of perjury, that the foregoing is true and correct this _____day of _____,19___ at _____

_____residing at_____

_____residing at_____

_____residing at_____

Comment: This is called the attestation clause. It's language establishes that the will was executed in the proper manner. In most states, the clause will serve not only to prove this point in probate court, but will also operate to "self-prove" the will (i.e. eliminate the need to produce a witness or an affidavit of the witness in court).

In certain other states (listed in Part 9), your will should be executed in front of a notary public if you wish it to be self-proving. This can be helpful if you are pretty sure that the value of your probate estate will result in formal probate proceedings (See Part 6).

WillWriter gives you the option of printing out your will in the form that allows for notarization. If you choose this option, WillWriter eliminates the "declaration under penalty of perjury language", adds some words to the main clause showing you are having your will notarized, and prints out the following statement after the main clause.

State of _____

County of _____

Subscribed, sworn to and acknowleged before me by _____, the testator, and _____, _____, and _____, witnesses, personally known to me (or proved to me on the basis of satisfactory evidence to be the persons), this ____ day of ____, 19____

Signed _____

_____
Official capacity of
officer

Remember, your will is still perfectly valid, even if you choose not to have it notarized. But, if you are resident of one of the states listed in Part 9, we believe that the convenience to you and your witnesses in not going to the notary is outweighed by the greater ease your executor will probably have in getting a notarized will admitted to probate, should formal probate be necessary.

One Last Note: Notarization does not eliminate the need for witnesses. Witnesses make your will valid. Notarization simply makes it easier to prove that the will is yours.

PART 14

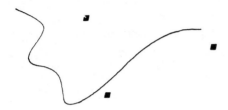

WillWriter User's Manual

A. Introduction

In the previous 13 parts of this manual, we covered a variety of legal topics relevant to making a valid and effective will. Here we shift gears a little and provide you with guidance on operating WillWriter as a computer program. Although WillWriter is designed to be "user friendly," we anticipate that many of you will have questions about the program that are not completely answered on the computer screens. Hopefully you will find your answers here.

Before we get into specifics, however, we wish to emphasize one obvious but important point. Making your will is a serious act and warrants sincere attempts by you to understand our instructions and to comply with them to the best of your ability. Thus, when the program asks you to name the beneficiary of a specific bequest without imposing any conditions, please just provide the name, with no additional comments. When you are asked to enter your name "the way you sign checks," please do so. Entering a nickname can lead to problems after your death. The point is, we have done our best to present you with complete information and instructions so that you can make a valid and effective will. It's your job to do your best to understand the information and follow the instructions. Okay, end of sermon. Thanks for listening. Let's get on with it.

EDITOR'S NOTE: Throughout the rest of this part, we frequently refer to specific commands and keys on your keyboard (e.g., Press "Return", Type "V", "Enter Information", etc). When we do, we usually enclose the reference in quotation marks. Do not get confused and think you should type the quotation marks as well as what is in them. They are only being used to set off the particular command or key being discussed. However, every rule has its exceptions and what we have said here is no different. For the rare occasion when we want you to type the quotation marks, we'll tell you.

B. Make Copies

Before you actually use WillWriter, you should make a backup copy of the program diskette. Apple users may do this by carefully taking the following steps:

1. Boot the WillWriter disk.

2. When the drive stops, interrupt the program by holding down the control key while pressing "Reset". This will result in the "]" symbol appearing on the screen.

3. Enter "CALL 48888", and press Return.

4. When another "]" appears on the screen, Enter "-FILER", and press Return.

5. When the ProDOS menu comes up, press "V" to select volume commands.

6. When the next menu comes up, press "C" to select "Copy a volume".

7. When the options appear, press "Return" to select the default slot (6).

8. Press "Return" to select the default drive (1).

9. Press "Return" to select the default slot for the copy (6).

10. If you have a second disk drive, press "Return" to select the default drive (2) for the copy. Then insert disks and press "Return".

11. If you have only one drive, you must select slot (1) again by typing "1" and "Return". Then, insert the source disk (i.e., WillWriter) and press "Return". The ProDOS copy routine will load a portion of the source disk into memory and then prompt you to insert the copy disk.

12. Whether you are using one disk or two disks, when the "New volume name" message comes up, press "Return" to select the default name LEGISOFT.

13. If your copy disk has not been previously formatted, it will be formatted at this time and the copying routine will proceed. If the copy disk has already been formatted under ProDOS or DOS, you will be asked whether you want to destroy all information on it. Press "Y" to proceed with the copy, which means existing information on the copy disk will be deleted (and the disk reformatted if the prior formatting was DOS), or press "N" to stop the copy routine and select another copy disk.

14. If you have only one drive, you will be prompted when to change disks. Always be sure

the drive has fully stopped before changing disks. The copying procedure will be very tedious, requiring about 10 changes of disks. This procedure alone has led to the purchase of a second disk drive by many Apple owners.

15. When the copying is done, press the ESC key (escape) twice to get to the FILER main menu. Select the option "Q" and you will return to the beginning of WillWriter if you have made your copy before using the program, as we suggest here. If you have already used WillWriter and have quit, you will be returned to where you were when you first started your copy.

NOTE FOR IBM USERS: Consult Section K ("IBM Notes") for how to make a copy.

C. Let's Get Started

For Apple computers:

1. Turn on the monitor.

2. Insert the WillWriter diskette in the disk drive.

3. Turn on the computer.

The program will then begin operating (i.e., "boot up"). If the computer is already on and you are running either of the Apple operating systems (i.e., DOS* or ProDOS*) as indicated by the appearance of the "]" symbol on the screen,

---

* DOS and ProDOS are trademarks of Apple Computer, Inc. WillWriter is a ProDOS program under license from Apple. You do not need to obtain ProDOS for your computer, however, as it is included on the WillWriter disk.

you can avoid turning the computer off and on again by typing "IN#6", followed by pressing the "Return" key. This and other ways to boot the disk are described in your Apple User's Manual.

For IBM computers:

1. Obtain "BASIC" from your system disk by typing Basic/S:240 and the carriage return key (sometimes called "Return").

2. Run the WillWriter program by typing the following, including the quotation mark, and then pressing "Return":

RUN "WW

3. If you are using Advanced BASIC, type RUN "WWA

Consult your IBM BASIC Manual and Section K of this Part for more details.

Regardless of which computer you are using, you should see an identification of the program for a brief time as the program is put into memory (i.e., "loads"). If you are unable to boot, check your system by booting another disk that you know works. Also, make sure your system is appropriate for WillWriter (see the last page of the manual). If your system works and is the right kind, return your disk to your dealer or to Nolo Press for a replacement.

D. Basic Outline of the Program

Here we give you the "big" picture of the program. We get into more specific details about the program's features in the following sections. In its most basic manifestation, WillWriter is a series of messages and questions in the form of "screens" that are displayed on your monitor. After you read each screen, you will be asked either to answer a question (usually "Yes" or "No"), or to enter some piece of information (such as the name of a person you want to leave property to), or to simply press the "Return" key to move to the next screen. When you are done with the screens, WillWriter will produce a valid and effective will containing the appropriate information and expressing your wishes.

Organizationally, WillWriter consists of four main parts in the following order:

1. An introduction to:

a. Wills generally;

b. The will you can write using Will-Writer; and

c. The basic instructions necessary to operate the program.

2. A series of questions that you answer in order to:

a. Provide the program with pertinent general information, such as your name, whether you are married, etc.; and

b. Indicate your choices about what property you want to leave, who you want to leave it to, who you want to choose for executor, who you wish to serve as guardian of your minor children, and so on;

3. An opportunity to review and change your previous entries. We have briefly discussed how this feature works in Part 12(B) ("Updating Your Will") and will do so in more detail in Section H of this part.

4. Specific instructions on readying your printer and printing out your will. Also, in

this part of the program you are provided the opportunity to:

    a. Return to the review process;

    b. Erase your will and start over; and

    c. Temporarily quit the program before you print your will. This might be appropriate if you can't completely review your will without getting more information.

"COME ON FOLKS - TAKE ME HOME
I'M USER FRIENDLY"

Now that you have some sense of how the WillWriter program works overall, it's time to turn to the details. The rest of this part contains the following information:

    1. General operational tips (Section E);

    2. Helpful program features (Section F);

3. Making lists of names and property under WillWriter (Section G);

4. How the WillWriter review (and update) process works (Section H);

5. How to print your will (Section I);

6. Representations of the program screens along with brief explanations and cross-references (Section J); and

7. Special notes for users of IBM and IBM-compatible computers (Section K).

E. Some General Tips on Running WillWriter

Tip 1: Use Your "Return" Key Only After Your Entry Is Completed

WillWriter asks you for two different types of input. Either you will be requested to select a choice (usually "Y" for yes or "N" for no) or to type in some information (such as your name). Either way, you should press the "Return" key only after your <u>entire</u> entry is completed. This is important especially where the information you want to enter takes up more than one line (for instance, when you are describing bequests). You may be tempted to press the "Return" key at the end of one line in order to move the cursor to the following one. Please don't do this. Pressing the "Return" key terminates the particular entry being worked on and signals the program that you are ready to go on to the next step. If you slipped up on this by pressing "Return" at the end of the line, just type "N" when you are asked to verify your entry. You will be returned for another try. This time remember to let the cursor go from one line to the next by itself.

Tip 2: Correct Information by Using the Back Arrow Key

You can correct information by using your "back arrow" key. Simply press this key until the error has been erased and then retype the correct information. Obviously you must do this before you press "Return" and move to the next screen. Of course, as we mentioned in Tip 1, you can undo a premature pressing of "Return" by simply typing "N" when you are asked to verify your previous entry. Then, you will be given another opportunity to erase and retype.

Tip 3: Don't Worry About Irregular Word Breaks

If your entry lasts more than one line, the program may break a word in the middle and continue it on the next line. Don't worry about this. When you print out your will, the word will be together in one piece. Similarly, you may be tempted to fill the space at the end of the line with spaces, thus bringing the cursor to the next line before you continue your entry. With WillWriter, however, the cursor will <u>auto-matically</u> go to the next line when the first is completed.

Tip 4: Using Semi-colons to Enter Information

To guarantee that your will has a visually pleasing appearance, there are times when you should use semicolons when entering information. This is because WillWriter recognizes a semi-colon placed between items of information as an instruction to print the information following the semicolon on a separate line. It is particularly appropriate to use semicolons when entering a person's name and address. For example, assume you want to enter both the name and the address of Horatio J. Fenster, your choice for executor. If you entered the information as

"Horatio J. Fenster;1024 Disk Dr.;Lost Wages,
Nevada", the information would be produced in
your will as follows:

                Horatio J. Fenster
                1024 Disk Dr.
                Lost Wages, Nevada

Without the semicolons, the information would
be printed exactly as you typed it (e.g., Horatio J. Fenster, 1024 Disk Dr., Lost Wages, Nevada). The information is validly entered in
your will, either way. The semicolons simply
improve appearance. It's entirely up to you.

NOTE: In our example above, we did not put
spaces either before or after the semicolons.
You don't need to either. If you do, however,
the only detriment will be cosmetic.

Residuary Estate and Real Estate Note: If
you specifically type in the names of two or
more people to receive "the rest of your personal property and/or your real estate, use the
semicolon to separate the names. If you provide
an address with the names, use a double semi-
colon (;;) between the last element of an address and the next name. Again, this is for
cosmetic purposes.

Tip 5: Do Not Interrupt Program or Touch Disk Drive While Drive Is Running

If the red light on the front of your drive
is on, or you hear a whirring sound, your drive
is running. If you remove a diskette during
this time, the file containing your will information may be destroyed and the program itself
damaged. Throughout the program, we provide you
with an opportunity to quit without losing information or doing damage, by simply entering
"Q". This will save the information you have
already provided and allow you to resume at that
point when you reboot the disk. Use this facil-
ity wherever appropriate. Remember, make sure
the red light is off and no sound is coming from
the drive before you remove the floppy.

Tip 6: Use WillWriter with the "Caps Lock" Down

Although it is possible to enter information in lower case (except with the Apple II+), we recommend that you use capital letters throughout. This will enhance the appearance of your printed will without sacrificing anything in performance. By keeping the "caps lock" key down from the beginning, you won't have to think about this during the rest of the program. Of course, if you prefer lower and upper case letters in your will, feel free to disregard our advice. For Apple II+ users, don't worry about the "caps lock" key. You don't have one. However, you won't need one because your computer only uses capital letters.

Tip 7: Distinguish the Letter "O" from the Number "0" and the Letter "I" from the Number "1"

Many users (even experienced ones) confuse the letter "O" with the number "0", and the letter "l" with the number "1". The result is that information entered is neither what is intended nor what the computer expects to receive. When using WillWriter, please keep these commonly blurred distinctions in mind.

Tip 8: Entering Information

Here are some pointers on entering names, descriptions of bequests, or other information.

1. Type in the information requested, the same as you would with a typewriter. But, unlike a typewriter, which requires you to manually press the "Return" key at the end of each line, the computer takes care of line returns without your intervention (Tip 3, above). In

other words, just keep typing until you're done.
Then press "Return".

   2. Read each screen carefully so you will
know what information or decision is being asked
for. Each screen is carefully worded so that
you can provide the correct response for that
part of the program.

   3. Provide only the information requested.
Thus, when you are asked to name your children,
don't use that space for other persons. When
you are asked to name a beneficiary to receive a
specific bequest, simply name the beneficiary
(and provide an address, if known). Don't add
additional phrases (such as, "but only if he
continues his marriage with my friend Sue," or
"but only if she sells her 1959 Volkswagen").
When you are told you can leave your real estate
to your spouse, your children, or any <u>one</u> person
or charity, don't name two different persons to
receive the real estate.

Tip 9: Understanding Truncated Screen Displays

   When requesting you to make lists (e.g., list
your children), WillWriter displays each list
entry you have made and gives you the option of
either changing it, adding new entries, or going
on to the next screen. Due to space limita-
tions, only the first part of the entry is
displayed. Don't think that WillWriter has lost
part of your entry, however. The full entry is
stored and will be printed out at the appropriate time. This is covered in more detail in
Section G, below.

Tip 10: For Commodore Users

   Don't press the Commodore + Shift keys together
or the screen will become garbled. To restore the
screen, press the Commodore + Shift keys again.

F. Some Specific General Features of WillWriter

The following features operate throughout the program until the point where you have completed your will and are ready to print it.

1. Top of Screen

The top line of each screen contains a brief description of the subject matter covered in the specific screen. Thus, the top line of the screen asking you for the names of your children appears as "CHILDREN'S NAMES".

2. Left Side of Screen

In the left-hand margin of the screen, there is a reference to a specific part of this manual. The referenced part of the manual contains useful and often necessary information about the material presented on the screen. This reference is also a reminder that the WillWriter program and manual are designed to be used together. Only by understanding the relevant material in the manual will you get the most out of WillWriter.

3. Bottom of Screen

The two lines in the bottom margin of each screen tell you which program options are available for that screen and what to do when you are through reading the screen or entering information (e.g., TYPE "Y" OR "NO" AND RETURN, TYPE REQUESTED INFORMATION AND THEN RETURN, PRESS "RETURN" TO GO TO NEXT SCREEN). Let's now take a closer look at these bottom-margin instructions and options.

a. "Yes" and "No"

WillWriter frequently asks you to answer a specific question (e.g., "Do you have children

under 18?") "Yes" or "No". The "Yes" and "No"
question is also used when you check information
already entered by you (e.g., "Is this correct?"). Either way, this is what you can expect to occur next:

● If you type "Y" and then press the "Return"
key, WillWriter saves your answer and moves to
the next screen.

● If you type "N" and "Return", you get
another chance to answer the question.

● If you forget to press the "Return" key,
the computer does nothing.

● If you give any answer other than "Y" or
"N" (unless you select one of the special options listed in the bottom margin), the computer
will beep and do nothing.

b. Press "Return" and Go to Next Screen

WillWriter makes frequent use of the "Return"
key. You must always press it to tell the
computer when you are ready to go from one
purely informational screen to the next screen.
In this situation, the screen will say "Press
Return And Go To The Next Screen."

c. Type Requested Information and
Then "Return"

WillWriter also makes frequent use of the
"Return" key to tell the computer you are finished providing information requested in a particular screen. In this instance, the screen
says "Type Requested Information and Then Return." After you have entered information (or
when you are backing up, or while you are reviewing your will after it is complete) and have
pressed "Return", you will again see the information you have just previously entered displayed on the screen. This time it will be
followed by the question, "Is this OK?". If you
say "N" (meaning it is not OK), you will then go

135

to a screen with the same information displayed
and the cursor flashing at the end of the text.
This gives you the chance to correct it by using
the "left arrow" key described earlier (see Tip
2, above).

d. Type "?" for Definitions of Legal Terms

By typing the "?" key, you may obtain a brief
on-screen definition of unfamiliar legal terms
being used in the particular screen being
viewed. The terms for which definitions are
provided are emphasized on the screen itself
through the use of capital letters and under-
lining. For example:

YOUR STATE GOES HERE

PROPERTY YOU CAN LEAVE BY WILL

Under the laws of NEW YORK, ←
your ESTATE consists of all property
which you own seperately (this
includes all property which you own
in your name alone) and your share
of property which you own as a
TENANT IN COMMON.

See manual Section 5.C.

PRESS "RETURN" TO GO TO NEXT SCREEN
(? = DEF B = BACK UP Q = QUIT * = WHERE?) 22

SEE MANUAL PART 5

If you desire a definition for any such term,
simply type "?". Each defined term will then
become highlighted and numbered. For example:

```
┌─────────────────────────────────────────────┐
│ S │ ¹PROPERTY YOU CAN LEAVE BY WILL           │
│ E │                                           │
│ E │   Under the laws of NEW YORK, ←           │
│   │   your ²ESTATE consists of all property   │
│ M │   which you own seperately (this          │
│ A │   includes all property which you own     │
│ N │   in your name alone) and your share      │
│ U │   of property which you own as a          │
│ A │                                           │
│ L │   ³TENANT IN COMMON.                      │
│   │      See manual Section 5.C.              │
│ P │ -------------------------------------     │
│ A │                                           │
│ R │   PRESS "RETURN" TO GO TO NEXT SCREEN      │
│ T │  (? = DEF  B = BACK UP  Q = QUIT  * = WHERE?) 22 │
│ 5 │                                           │
└─────────────────────────────────────────────┘
```

By typing next the number of the term you want
defined and then (as always) pressing "Return",
the definition (and often a cross-reference to
the manual) will appear. When you are done
reading it, press the "Return" key. You will be
returned to the screen where the defined terms
are highlighted and numbered. If there are
additional highlighted terms that you want defined, simply select the appropriate number and
press "Return".

     When you desire to leave the screen with the
highlighted and numbered terms and return to the
main program, simply press "Return." You will
come back to the screen you were on before you
ever pushed "?" in the first place. You may
then continue as if you hadn't asked for a
definition. By the way, you can skip one step
if you are done reading a definition and do not

want to see any other definition on that screen. For Apple & IBM simply press the "escape" (ESC) key and you will return to the normal screen. For Commodore use the left arrow key.

e. Type "B" for Back Up

There will be times when you desire to go back to a previous question to check your answer or change information. Although you are provided an opportunity to do this near the end of the program under a master menu of most program sections (we call it the "review" screen), it is also usually possible to back up a screen at a time while still in the main part of WillWriter. You do this by typing "B" and then "Return", assuming the "B" option appears at the bottom of the screen. Each screen that you back up to displays your previous answer and then asks you, "Is this OK"? If you type "N" and "Return," you are able to change your answer. If you type "Y" and "Return", your previous answer remains and you go forward. If you again type "B" and "Return", instead of "Y" or "N", you back up to the previous screen.

If the "B" option does not appear at the bottom of the screen, this means you cannot back up from that screen. To get around this, finish your entry and type "Y" (and "Return") when asked whether the entry is okay as is. This takes you forward to the next screen. If that screen has the "B" option, then simply back up to where you wish to go, one screen at a time.

In some instances, the next screen also does not have the "B" option. This may occur, for example, when you enter the part of the program where you are asked to leave specific bequests to specific beneficiaries. Once you begin that sequence, you may have to advance through several screens to reach the "B" option.

All of this probably seems a little cumbersome. Fortunately, if the reason you want to back up is to review a portion of your work (e.g., the bequests you have made, and to whom you have made them), there is a better alterna-

tive than backing up. We detail this alternative in Section H, below.

We recognize that the back-up option may seem
a little confusing at times. For example, suppose you want to use the "B" option at a time
when the screen is asking you for information.
If you have not yet entered any information and
type "B", the "B" appears on the screen in the
space where you would otherwise be entering the
information. Don't worry. When you then press
"Return", the program interprets the single "B"
as a request to back up, rather than as the
requested information.

What happens, however, if you want to back
up after you have entered some information? In
that case, simply press the "left arrow" key
repeatedly to erase any information you have
already entered. Then type "B" and press "Return". As we mentioned earlier, you first see a
"B" appear where the program was expecting information, and then the previous screen appears.

NOTE: If you make certain changes after
having backed up, you may encounter some new
information or questions which have now become
appropriate because of your changes. For example, if you originally said you had no spouse,
but later back up to that section and change
your answer to the affirmative, you then encounter some new screens dealing with leaving property to spouses. See Section H, below.

f. Type "Q" for Quit

There may be times when you want to stop in
the middle of writing your will and store what
you've done without having to start again at the
beginning. Or, you may wish to store your information on disk in the event of a power or
other failure. If you type "Q", WillWriter
first stores the information already entered on
the disk and then asks you whether you really
want to quit for now. If you then type "Y", you
get your wish. If you type "C", however, for
"continue", you are returned to where you were.

Once you have quit, you will probably need to "reboot" the program to start it working again. When you do, you are returned to the place where you left off. Thus, by using "Q" you can quit without wasting the time you already devoted to making out your will.

g. Type "*" for Where Am I?

As you surely understand by now, using Will-Writer is a linear process. That is, you are asked a series of questions all of which lead up to the final result--a valid and effective will. Because at some point you will probably want to get your bearings relative to the entire process, we have provided a means to do this. Simply type "*" when the bottom margin indicates this feature is available (it is in most screens). In this case, typing "Return" is not necessary. You instantly leave what you are doing, even if you are in the middle of entering information, and see a display of all of the sections of the program. The sections that you have completed will be marked with an asterisk (*). An arrow will point to your current location.

When using this feature, you may notice that some earlier parts of the program are not marked with an asterisk. That is because these parts of the program were not appropriate (relevant) to your situation. For example, if you do not have a spouse, several parts of the program dealing with spouses are skipped in your case and, accordingly, are not asterisked.

G. Making Lists of Names and Property Under WillWriter

At different places in the program, Will-Writer asks you to list:

- Your children;

- Any children of a deceased child; and

• Specific bequests of personal property to individuals or institutions.

Anticipating that you will want to be kept abreast of what you have already put in the list, and to have an opportunity to make deletions or corrections, WillWriter provides you with these options. Also, as briefly mentioned in Tip 9, above, WillWriter presents you with an abbreviated version of your prior list entries. For example, assuming you affirmatively answer WillWriter's question as to whether you have any children, you then see a screen that asks you to enter the name of the first child (the actual order doesn't matter--just that you get them all in). After entering the name and verifying it in the usual way, you then see a summary list of the names (at this point, this obviously only consists of the single child you just entered). If the name is too long for the space in the summary list, it is shortened (truncated). You are informed of this by a [+] sign and a note on the screen telling you that the name has been "Shortened for Display Only". Don't worry, the name is still stored in full in the computer's memory and will be properly printed out when you actually print your will.

Now for the major list-making options offered by WillWriter.

1. "A" for "Add More Names"

If you wish to add another name (or bequest) to the list, type "A" and "Return". You may have a maximum of 16 entries in any of these lists.

2. "R" for "Review Any Previous Entries in This List"

If you wish to review (or change) one of your previous entries on the list, type "R" and "Return". This is a way to see the entry in full, and is particularly useful for the list of bequests, where only limited information (the

first 16 characters of the name of the beneficiary and of the description of the bequest)
appears in the summary list. In fact, alternative beneficiaries do not appear at all. Thus,
this option allows you to see what property you
have described in any particular bequest or the
full name of the person (or alternate) to whom
you have left such property. If there is only
one entry on the list, you go directly to a
screen that contains the full entry and are
asked if the entry is okay, or whether you want
to change it. If there is more than one entry,
you are asked to select the number of the one
you want to review or change.

NOTE: As we mentioned in our earlier discussion on backing up, when you want to check and
perhaps change an entry in a list, this review
utility is much more effective than using the
"B" option. Thus, if in the middle of leaving
specific bequests you decide you want to see
what you've already left, simply advance forward
until you reach the screen providing the "R"
option and then select the appropriate entry for
review.

3. "D" for "Delete Any Previous Entries in This List"

The "D" entry works much the same as "R",
only the entire entry is eliminated. In the
children or grandchildren lists, the space left
by deleting is closed up and the list then has
one fewer entry. For the bequests, this space
is left open; you may fill it up later by using
the "R" option on this space. But no harm is
done by leaving the space open, since the section of the program that prints your will simply
ignores any space that is blank because of deletions or because of an initial failure to enter
both a beneficiary and a description of the
bequest.

4. "Y" for "Yes, I Want to Quit"

To quit making the list and advance to a new

section of the program, type "Y" and "Return". This is what you choose when you are either satisfied with the list as it stands or plan on coming back to it later. If you don't return to make changes, WillWriter will consider the list complete and print all of the information contained in it.

Again, to select any of the options just discussed, simply type the appropriate letter ("A", "R", "D" or "Y") and "Return".

H. Reviewing Your Will

In our discussion in Part 12 (B) on updating your will, we briefly described how you can review and change portions of your will after you have completed the program. Here we cover this subject in more detail.

After the question and answer portion of WillWriter is completed, you are presented with a screen that lists each portion of the program and asks you whether you care to go back and review any of your answers. If you do, you are told to type the number that directly adjoins the portion to be reviewed. Here is a sample of that screen.

```
REVIEW/MODIFY YOUR WILL:
S
E   BASICS:      1. Name
E                2. State
M                3. County
A                4. Married?
N                5. Spouse's name
U                6. Facts about Children
A
L   BEQUESTS:    7. Personal Property
                 8. Real estate
P                9. The rest
A                10. Exclude Children?
R
T   NOMINATE:    11. Guardian
                 12. Guardian of estate
1                13. Executor
4   Type the number of any item you want to
    review or change: ▓_ & "Return"
    - - - - - - - - - - - - - - - - - - - - - - - -
    PRESS "RETURN" TO GO TO NEXT SCREEN
        (? = DEF    Q = QUIT    * = WHERE?)    [41]
```

For most of these portions, when you type the number, you go directly to the desired item, where you are provided an opportunity to review your answers, make desired changes, and then return directly to the review screen. However, for a few portions the review process works a little differently. When you desire to review your entries for

● your state,

● your marital status,

● basic facts about your children,

● who you left your real estate to,

● who you left "the rest of your property" to,

you will go directly to these items the same as with the other items. But, if you decide to make some changes, you will be shown a message telling you that any changes in that section will require you to review your prior answers to the portions of the program that come after that item, and maybe to answer some new questions not presented earlier.

Put differently, once you make a change in one of these items, you do not return directly to the review screen, but instead must proceed through the rest of the program (reviewing your previous answers and encountering new questions) until you reach the review screen again.

Why does the program work this way in respect to these particular items? Simply put, changes in these items logically require you to recon-sider previous answers and to consider new ques-tions. For example, suppose you have your first child, and therefore decide to make a new will incorporating this fact. You will need to go back and change your answers to the questions about whether you have children and whether any such children are below 18 years of age. Be-cause you did not have children before, Will-Writer did not ask you to name them and did not request that you name a guardian. Now, however, your answer requires that you name the child and that you reflect on the potential need for a guardian. Accordingly, WillWriter brings you up through the program so that these new items can now be presented for your consideration. Although making changes in these items clearly involves a burden on you, the user, we believe that the security you will gain by knowing that your will is legally valid and effective is well worth it.

I. Printing Your Will

Now that you have finished reviewing and changing your entries, you will want to print your will. Simply pressing "Return" will take you from the review screen to a final screen that presents you with the following options:

"P" and "Return" for print;

"R" and "Return" for review (this takes you back to the review screen);

"E" and "Return" to erase your will and start over;

"Q" and "Return" for quit;

You should type "P" and "Return". You will then be presented with a brief delay and a message telling you to ready your printer. Any printer that works with your computer will work with WillWriter.

The first screen in the printing program asks you whether you plan to have your will notarized. Although notarization is not required to make a valid will, it will make it easier to have the will admitted to probate in some states. See Part 11, Sec. A.

The next screen asks you whether you want to see your will on the screen rather than print it on paper. You will be able to do this only if you have an 80 column display (it must be in slot

#3 if you have an Apple II+ or IIe). If you
don't it is just as well to print out a draft
copy which you can then check for errors. In the
IBM version, in addition to being able to view
the will on the screen prior to printing it, you
can see the will on the screen as it is printed
on paper.

The next message asks you whether you are
using continuous paper or single sheets. Type
"C" and "Return" for continuous paper or "S" and
"Return" for single sheet. You can use the
single sheet option even though you are using
continuous paper.

You will next be told that the program is set
to print 58 lines per page and will be asked if
this is okay. If it is, type "Y" and "Return".
If you wish to print with fewer lines per page,
type "N" and "Return". You will then be asked
to enter the number of lines you prefer. If you
choose another number, you will then be asked to
verify that number.

NOTE: What if you don't know how many lines
your printer prints per page? Although most
printers print 58 lines to the page, yours may
not. The best approach is to select the 58 line
default (i.e., type "Y" when asked whether 58
lines is okay) and then print your will. If
there is too large a space at the bottom, increase the number. If the space is too small,
or you have run over onto the next page, reduce
the number. Nothing succeeds like trial and
error.

After you have selected the number of lines
per page, you are asked (on the Apple II+ and
IIc versions) if your printer is connected to
slot #1 (it almost always is). Type "Y" and
"Return" if it is. Type "N" and "Return" if it
is not. Then, change the slot number. If you
are using an IBM computer, turn to "IBM Notes"
in Section K.

Finally, you are asked if you are ready to
print. If you type "Y", you will begin to

146

print. If you type "N", you will be able to go
back and reset your print options (e.g., lines
per page). Once the will begins to print, it
will continue until completed. There is no
escape. However, since your will is unlikely to
be more than five pages, this should not prove
too great a hardship.

CAUTION FOR APPLE USERS: If your printer is
not attached or turned on when you begin to
print, the WillWriter program may hang up (or
"go to lunch" in hacker lingo). If this happens, ready your printer and then press the
"control" key and the reset button. You will
then be presented with the proDOS prompt "]".
Now type Run and press Return. You will be
returned to the options menu ("P", "R", "E",
"Q").

CAUTION FOR IBM USERS: See "IBM Notes" in
Section K, below.

CAUTION FOR COMMODORE USERS: When printing you will
be asked whether the printer needs true ASCII. If you
are not sure, say "no" and use Pet ASCII. If you've
made the wrong choice and get nonsense printing, press
the RUN/STOP key, enter "Return" and make the alternate
selection.

J. The WillWriter Program Screen by Screen

Now that we have covered the nuts and bolts
of operating the WillWriter program, it is time
to look at the actual major screens that Will-
Writer uses, along with brief explanatory comments. Many of you may wish to skip this section for now and proceed directly to the program. Others, however, will want to review the
screens in printed form before actually touching
the keys. If any of you become somewhat confused about a particular screen while using
WillWriter, you can locate the numbered screen
in this section by looking at the number at the
lower right corner of the program screen.

NOTE: Each screen of the WillWriter program
is numbered. Since we do not reproduce every
screen, however, but only the major ones, the
screens you find in this section will often jump
numbers (e.g., you will go from screen 20 to
screen 24).

YOUR NAME

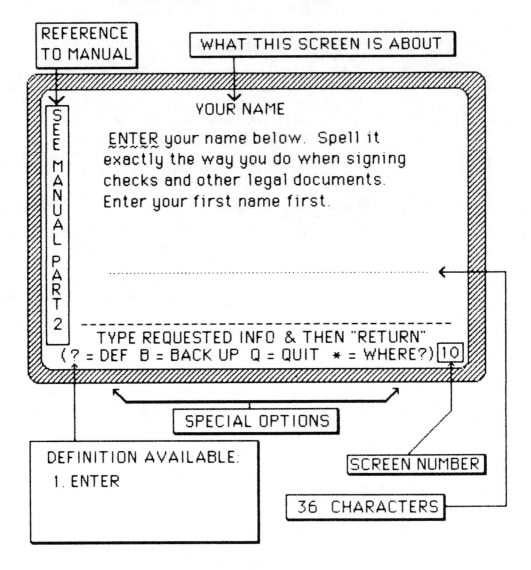

REFERENCE
TO MANUAL

WHAT THIS SCREEN IS ABOUT

SEE MANUAL PART 2

YOUR NAME

ENTER your name below. Spell it
exactly the way you do when signing
checks and other legal documents.
Enter your first name first.

TYPE REQUESTED INFO & THEN "RETURN"
(? = DEF   B = BACK UP   Q = QUIT   * = WHERE?) 10

SPECIAL OPTIONS

DEFINITION AVAILABLE:
 1. ENTER

SCREEN NUMBER

36 CHARACTERS

YOUR STATE

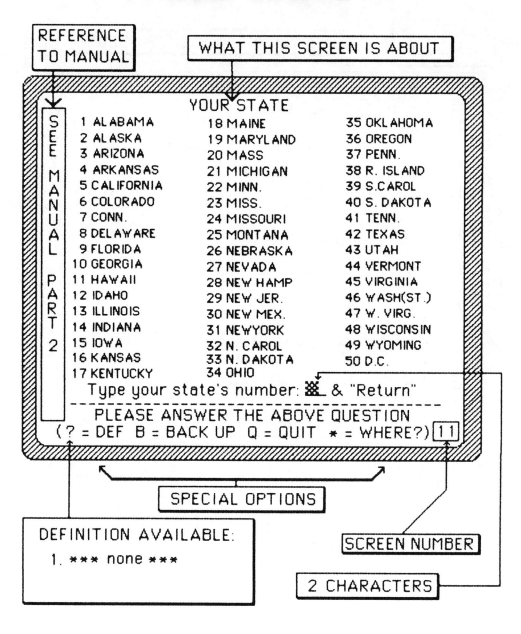

REFERENCE TO MANUAL

WHAT THIS SCREEN IS ABOUT

YOUR STATE

S E E   M A N U A L   P A R T   2

1 ALABAMA	18 MAINE	35 OKLAHOMA
2 ALASKA	19 MARYLAND	36 OREGON
3 ARIZONA	20 MASS	37 PENN.
4 ARKANSAS	21 MICHIGAN	38 R. ISLAND
5 CALIFORNIA	22 MINN.	39 S.CAROL
6 COLORADO	23 MISS.	40 S. DAKOTA
7 CONN.	24 MISSOURI	41 TENN.
8 DELAWARE	25 MONTANA	42 TEXAS
9 FLORIDA	26 NEBRASKA	43 UTAH
10 GEORGIA	27 NEVADA	44 VERMONT
11 HAWAII	28 NEW HAMP	45 VIRGINIA
12 IDAHO	29 NEW JER.	46 WASH(ST.)
13 ILLINOIS	30 NEW MEX.	47 W. VIRG.
14 INDIANA	31 NEWYORK	48 WISCONSIN
15 IOWA	32 N. CAROL	49 WYOMING
16 KANSAS	33 N. DAKOTA	50 D.C.
17 KENTUCKY	34 OHIO	

Type your state's number: ▓▓ & "Return"

- -

PLEASE ANSWER THE ABOVE QUESTION

(? = DEF B = BACK UP Q = QUIT * = WHERE?) 11

SPECIAL OPTIONS

DEFINITION AVAILABLE:
1. *** none ***

SCREEN NUMBER

2 CHARACTERS

YOUR COUNTY

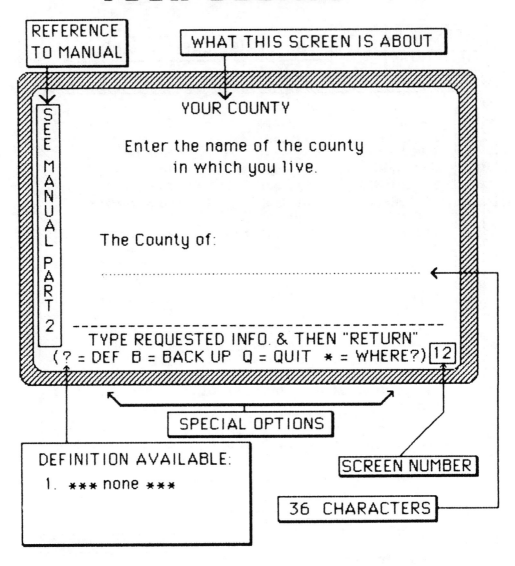

REFERENCE TO MANUAL

WHAT THIS SCREEN IS ABOUT

SEE MANUAL PART 2

YOUR COUNTY

Enter the name of the county
in which you live.

The County of:

....

- -
TYPE REQUESTED INFO. & THEN "RETURN"
(? = DEF B = BACK UP Q = QUIT * = WHERE?) 12

SPECIAL OPTIONS

DEFINITION AVAILABLE:
1. *** none ***

SCREEN NUMBER

36 CHARACTERS

MARRIED?

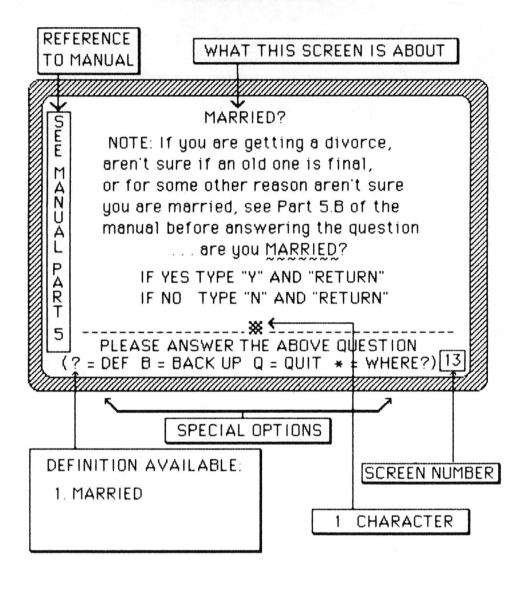

REFERENCE TO MANUAL

WHAT THIS SCREEN IS ABOUT

SEE MANUAL PART 5

MARRIED?

NOTE: If you are getting a divorce,
aren't sure if an old one is final,
or for some other reason aren't sure
you are married, see Part 5.B of the
manual before answering the question
... are you MARRIED?

IF YES TYPE "Y" AND "RETURN"
IF NO   TYPE "N" AND "RETURN"

PLEASE ANSWER THE ABOVE QUESTION
(? = DEF B = BACK UP Q = QUIT * = WHERE?) 13

SPECIAL OPTIONS

DEFINITION AVAILABLE:
1. MARRIED

SCREEN NUMBER

1 CHARACTER

YOUR SPOUSE'S NAME

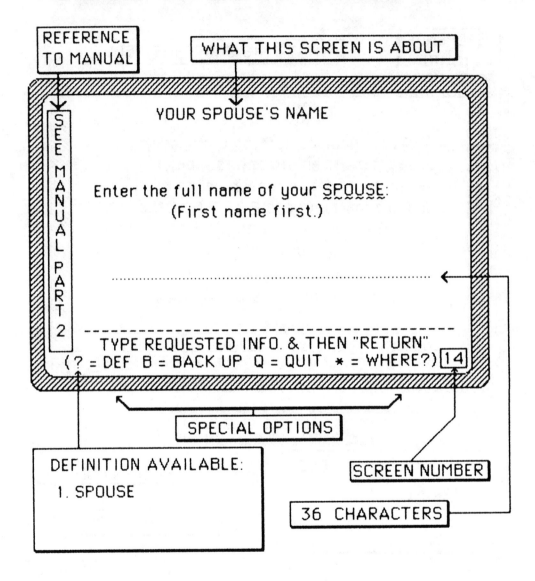

REFERENCE TO MANUAL

WHAT THIS SCREEN IS ABOUT

SEE MANUAL PART 2

YOUR SPOUSE'S NAME

Enter the full name of your SPOUSE:
(First name first.)

....

TYPE REQUESTED INFO. & THEN "RETURN"
(? = DEF B = BACK UP Q = QUIT * = WHERE?) [14]

SPECIAL OPTIONS

DEFINITION AVAILABLE:
1. SPOUSE

SCREEN NUMBER

36 CHARACTERS

CHILDREN?

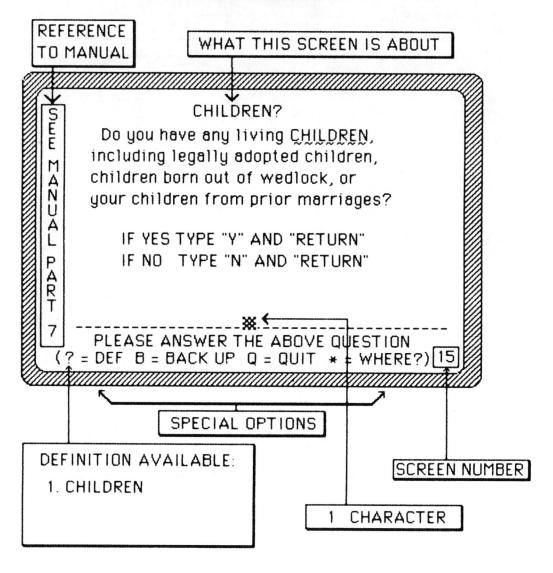

REFERENCE TO MANUAL

WHAT THIS SCREEN IS ABOUT

SEE MANUAL PART 7

CHILDREN?

Do you have any living CHILDREN, including legally adopted children, children born out of wedlock, or your children from prior marriages?

IF YES TYPE "Y" AND "RETURN"
IF NO TYPE "N" AND "RETURN"

※ ←

PLEASE ANSWER THE ABOVE QUESTION
(? = DEF B = BACK UP Q = QUIT * = WHERE?) 15

SPECIAL OPTIONS

DEFINITION AVAILABLE:
1. CHILDREN

SCREEN NUMBER

1 CHARACTER

CHILDREN'S NAMES

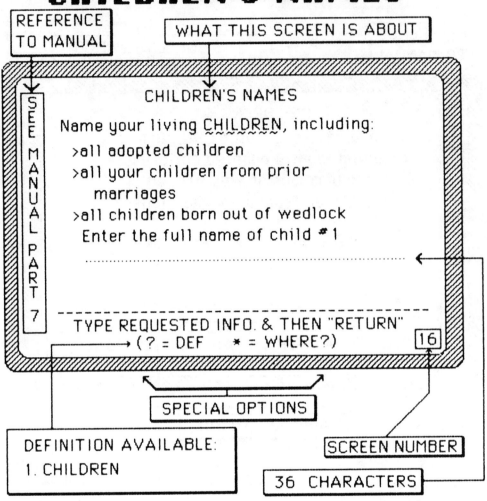

REFERENCE
TO MANUAL

WHAT THIS SCREEN IS ABOUT

SEE MANUAL PART 7

CHILDREN'S NAMES

Name your living CHILDREN, including:
  >all adopted children
  >all your children from prior
    marriages
  >all children born out of wedlock
  Enter the full name of child #1

....

- -
TYPE REQUESTED INFO. & THEN "RETURN"
→ (? = DEF   * = WHERE?)   16

SPECIAL OPTIONS

DEFINITION AVAILABLE:
1. CHILDREN

SCREEN NUMBER

36 CHARACTERS

NOTE: After naming each child, and verifying the name,
you will be given the following "menu" of choices:

TYPE "A" - TO ADD ANOTHER CHILD
     "R" - TO REVIEW OR CHANGE ONE
     "D" - TO DELETE ONE
     "Y" - IF LIST IS OK AS IS

Use "A" until you have named all your children.
Use "R" and "D" to correct errors.
Use "Y" to signify that you are done naming your children.

CHILDREN UNDER 18?

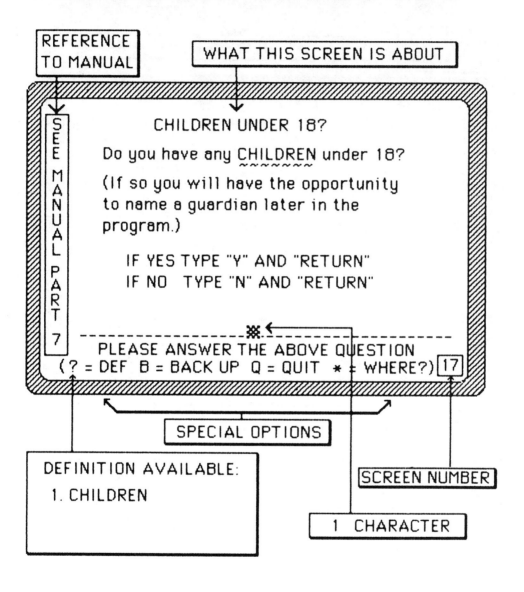

REFERENCE TO MANUAL

WHAT THIS SCREEN IS ABOUT

SEE MANUAL PART 7

CHILDREN UNDER 18?

Do you have any CHILDREN under 18?

(If so you will have the opportunity to name a guardian later in the program.)

IF YES TYPE "Y" AND "RETURN"
IF NO   TYPE "N" AND "RETURN"

PLEASE ANSWER THE ABOVE QUESTION
(? = DEF B = BACK UP Q = QUIT * = WHERE?) 17

SPECIAL OPTIONS

DEFINITION AVAILABLE:
1. CHILDREN

SCREEN NUMBER

1 CHARACTER

DECEASED CHILDREN?

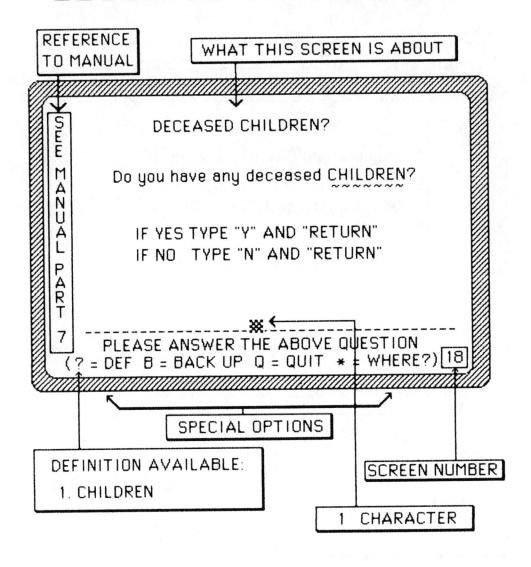

REFERENCE TO MANUAL

WHAT THIS SCREEN IS ABOUT

SEE MANUAL PART 7

DECEASED CHILDREN?

Do you have any deceased CHILDREN?
~~~~~~~

IF YES TYPE "Y" AND "RETURN"
IF NO TYPE "N" AND "RETURN"

PLEASE ANSWER THE ABOVE QUESTION
(? = DEF B = BACK UP Q = QUIT * = WHERE?) 18

SPECIAL OPTIONS

DEFINITION AVAILABLE:
1. CHILDREN

SCREEN NUMBER

1 CHARACTER

GRANDCHILDREN

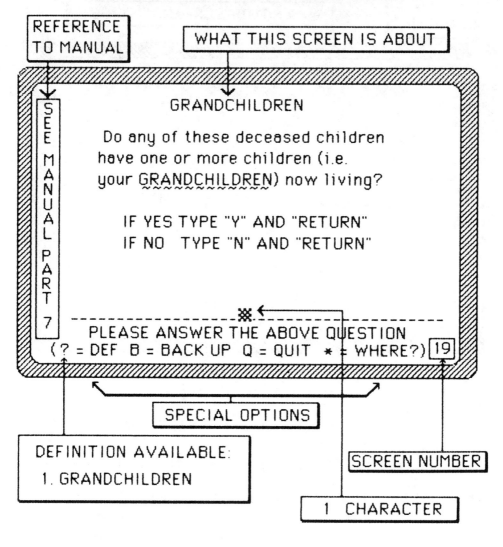

REFERENCE TO MANUAL

WHAT THIS SCREEN IS ABOUT

SEE MANUAL PART 7

GRANDCHILDREN

Do any of these deceased children
have one or more children (i.e.
your GRANDCHILDREN) now living?

IF YES TYPE "Y" AND "RETURN"
IF NO TYPE "N" AND "RETURN"

PLEASE ANSWER THE ABOVE QUESTION
(? = DEF B = BACK UP Q = QUIT * = WHERE?) 19

SPECIAL OPTIONS

DEFINITION AVAILABLE:
 1. GRANDCHILDREN

SCREEN NUMBER

1 CHARACTER

157

NAME CHILDREN OF DECEASED CHILDREN

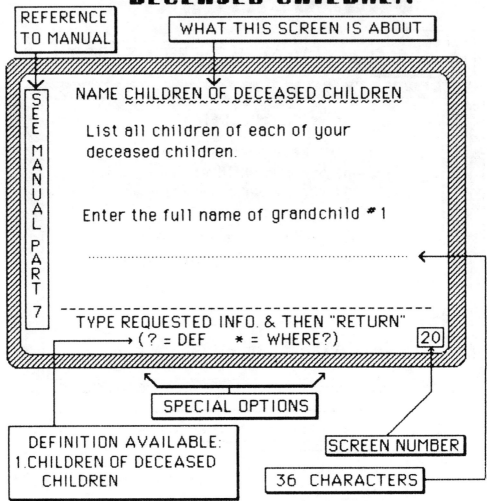

REFERENCE TO MANUAL

WHAT THIS SCREEN IS ABOUT

SEE MANUAL PART 7

NAME CHILDREN OF DECEASED CHILDREN

List all children of each of your deceased children.

Enter the full name of grandchild # 1

....

TYPE REQUESTED INFO. & THEN "RETURN"
(? = DEF   * = WHERE?)

20

SPECIAL OPTIONS

DEFINITION AVAILABLE:
1.CHILDREN OF DECEASED CHILDREN

SCREEN NUMBER

36 CHARACTERS

NOTE: Name all such grandchildren, one at a time. As when naming children you will see this menu:

```
TYPE "A" - TO ADD ANOTHER GRANDCHILD
      "R" - TO REVIEW OR CHANGE ONE
      "D" - TO DELETE ONE
      "Y" - IF LIST IS OK AS IS
```

Use "A" until you have named all.

Use "R" and "D" to correct errors.

Use "Y" to signify that you are done.

BEQUESTS OF PERSONAL PROPERTY

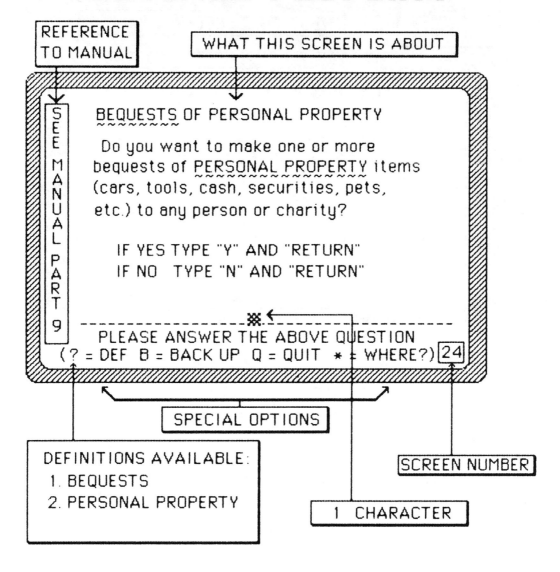

REFERENCE TO MANUAL

WHAT THIS SCREEN IS ABOUT

SEE MANUAL PART 9

BEQUESTS OF PERSONAL PROPERTY

Do you want to make one or more bequests of PERSONAL PROPERTY items (cars, tools, cash, securities, pets, etc.) to any person or charity?

IF YES TYPE "Y" AND "RETURN"
IF NO   TYPE "N" AND "RETURN"

----------------------- ※← ---------------

PLEASE ANSWER THE ABOVE QUESTION
(? = DEF B = BACK UP Q = QUIT * = WHERE?) 24

SPECIAL OPTIONS

DEFINITIONS AVAILABLE:
1. BEQUESTS
2. PERSONAL PROPERTY

SCREEN NUMBER

1 CHARACTER

159

PERSON TO RECEIVE THE BEQUEST

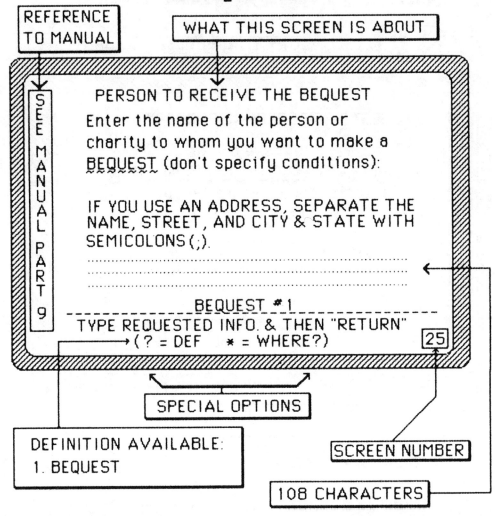

REFERENCE TO MANUAL

WHAT THIS SCREEN IS ABOUT

SEE MANUAL PART 9

PERSON TO RECEIVE THE BEQUEST

Enter the name of the person or charity to whom you want to make a BEQUEST (don't specify conditions):

IF YOU USE AN ADDRESS, SEPARATE THE NAME, STREET, AND CITY & STATE WITH SEMICOLONS (;).

....
....
....

––––––––––––––––––– BEQUEST #1 –––––––––––––––––––
TYPE REQUESTED INFO. & THEN "RETURN"
(? = DEF   * = WHERE?)   25

SPECIAL OPTIONS

DEFINITION AVAILABLE:
1. BEQUEST

SCREEN NUMBER

108 CHARACTERS

NOTE: This and the next two screens allow you to name the recipient of, describe, and name an alternate for, a series of up to 16 bequests of personal property. You cannot back up or quit until all three items are entered for a given bequest, but you can then review, change, or delete any of your bequests using the same menu described for screens 16 and 20.

DESCRIPTION OF BEQUEST

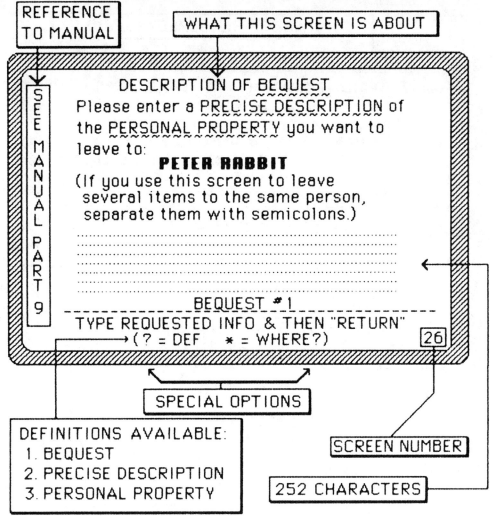

REFERENCE TO MANUAL

WHAT THIS SCREEN IS ABOUT

SEE MANUAL PART 9

DESCRIPTION OF BEQUEST
Please enter a PRECISE DESCRIPTION of the PERSONAL PROPERTY you want to leave to:
PETER RABBIT
(If you use this screen to leave several items to the same person, separate them with semicolons.)

BEQUEST #1
TYPE REQUESTED INFO & THEN "RETURN"
(? = DEF   * = WHERE?)
26

SPECIAL OPTIONS

DEFINITIONS AVAILABLE:
1. BEQUEST
2. PRECISE DESCRIPTION
3. PERSONAL PROPERTY

SCREEN NUMBER

252 CHARACTERS

NOTE: You may leave several items to the same person; using semicolons will improve the appearance of your printed will. If you need more space than is available here, you can leave a second bequest (perhaps also consisting of several items) to the same person.

ALTERNATE BENEFICIARY

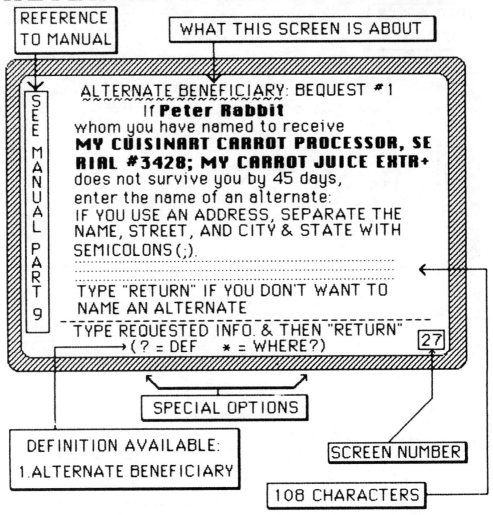

REFERENCE TO MANUAL

WHAT THIS SCREEN IS ABOUT

SEE MANUAL PART 9

ALTERNATE BENEFICIARY: BEQUEST #1
If **Peter Rabbit**
whom you have named to receive
**MY CUISINART CARROT PROCESSOR, SE
RIAL #3428; MY CARROT JUICE EXTR+**
does not survive you by 45 days,
enter the name of an alternate:
IF YOU USE AN ADDRESS, SEPARATE THE
NAME, STREET, AND CITY & STATE WITH
SEMICOLONS (;).

TYPE "RETURN" IF YOU DON'T WANT TO
NAME AN ALTERNATE

TYPE REQUESTED INFO. & THEN "RETURN"
→ (? = DEF   * = WHERE?)

27

SPECIAL OPTIONS

DEFINITION AVAILABLE:
1. ALTERNATE BENEFICIARY

SCREEN NUMBER

108 CHARACTERS

NOTE: Naming the alternate, which is optional, completes
a bequest (beneficiary, description, & alternate beneficiary). You will then be given the same menu as
described for screens 16 and 20.

REAL ESTATE

REFERENCE TO MANUAL

WHAT THIS SCREEN IS ABOUT

SEE MANUAL PART 9

REAL ESTATE

Leave all your REAL ESTATE to:

TYPE "C" TO NAME CHILDREN EQUALLY
OR TYPE "S" TO NAME YOUR SPOUSE
OR NAME ANY ONE PERSON OR CHARITY

IF YOU USE AN ADDRESS, SEPARATE THE
NAME, STREET, AND CITY & STATE WITH
SEMICOLONS (;).

....
....
....

TYPE REQUESTED INFO. & THEN "RETURN"
(? = DEF B = BACK UP Q = QUIT * = WHERE?) 28

SPECIAL OPTIONS

DEFINITION AVAILABLE:
1. REAL ESTATE

SCREEN NUMBER

108 CHARACTERS

NOTE: Options "S" and "C", which appear only if you are married and have children, respectively, allow you to name your spouse or your children (to share equally). WillWriter interprets any other entry as naming a person or institution--usually charitable.

163

ALTERNATE BENEFICIARY: REAL ESTATE

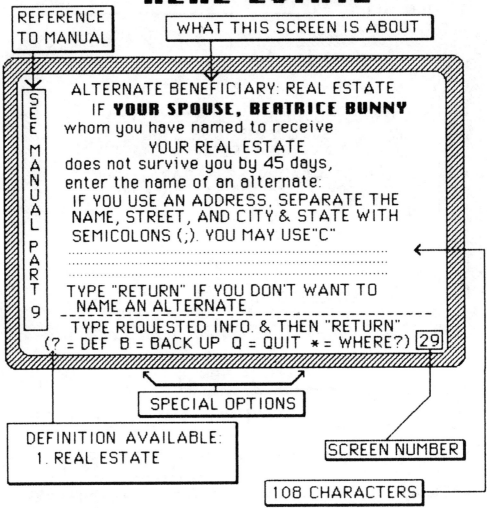

REFERENCE TO MANUAL

WHAT THIS SCREEN IS ABOUT

SEE MANUAL PART 9

ALTERNATE BENEFICIARY: REAL ESTATE
IF YOUR SPOUSE, BEATRICE BUNNY
whom you have named to receive
YOUR REAL ESTATE
does not survive you by 45 days,
enter the name of an alternate:
IF YOU USE AN ADDRESS, SEPARATE THE
NAME, STREET, AND CITY & STATE WITH
SEMICOLONS (;). YOU MAY USE"C"
....
....
TYPE "RETURN" IF YOU DON'T WANT TO
NAME AN ALTERNATE
TYPE REQUESTED INFO. & THEN "RETURN"
(? = DEF B = BACK UP Q = QUIT * = WHERE?) 29

SPECIAL OPTIONS

DEFINITION AVAILABLE:
1. REAL ESTATE

SCREEN NUMBER

108 CHARACTERS

NOTE: Options "S" and "C" have the same meaning as they did on the previous screen. In this sample the testator's spouse was named the primary beneficiary, so the choices remaining are to name the children (by typing "C" and "Return") or another person or charity.

164

REMAINING PROPERTY

REFERENCE TO MANUAL

WHAT THIS SCREEN IS ABOUT

SEE MANUAL PART 9

REMAINING PROPERTY

Leave the rest of your PROPERTY to:

TYPE "C" TO NAME CHILDREN EQUALLY
OR TYPE "S" TO NAME YOUR SPOUSE
OR NAME ANY ONE PERSON OR CHARITY

IF YOU USE AN ADDRESS, SEPARATE THE
NAME, STREET, AND CITY & STATE WITH
SEMICOLONS (;).

....
....
....

(Do this even if you think you have
disposed of all of your property.)

TYPE REQUESTED INFO. & THEN "RETURN"
(? = DEF   B = BACK UP   Q = QUIT   * = WHERE?) 30

SPECIAL OPTIONS

DEFINITION AVAILABLE:
  1. PROPERTY

SCREEN NUMBER

108 CHARACTERS

NOTE: Options "S" and "C", which appear only if you are married and have children, respectively, allow you to name your spouse or your children (to share equally). WillWriter interprets any other entry as naming a person or institution--usually charitable.

ALTERNATE BENEFICIARY: REST OF PROPERTY

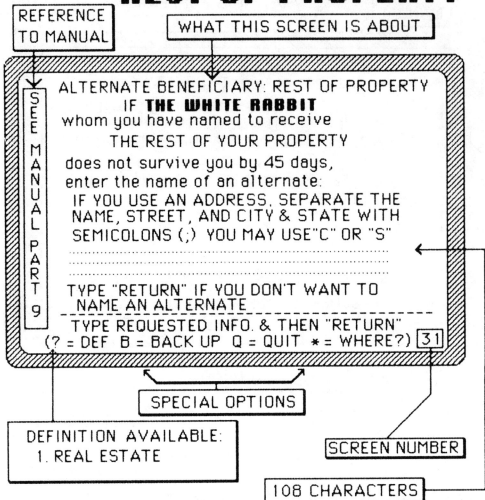

REFERENCE TO MANUAL

WHAT THIS SCREEN IS ABOUT

SEE MANUAL PART 9

ALTERNATE BENEFICIARY: REST OF PROPERTY
IF THE WHITE RABBIT
whom you have named to receive
THE REST OF YOUR PROPERTY
does not survive you by 45 days,
enter the name of an alternate:
IF YOU USE AN ADDRESS, SEPARATE THE
NAME, STREET, AND CITY & STATE WITH
SEMICOLONS (;) YOU MAY USE "C" OR "S"
....
....
....
TYPE "RETURN" IF YOU DON'T WANT TO
NAME AN ALTERNATE
TYPE REQUESTED INFO. & THEN "RETURN"
(? = DEF B = BACK UP Q = QUIT * = WHERE?) 31

SPECIAL OPTIONS

DEFINITION AVAILABLE:
1. REAL ESTATE

SCREEN NUMBER

108 CHARACTERS

NOTE: Options "S" and "C" have the same meaning as they did on the previous screen.

166

EXCLUDE SOME CHILDREN?

REFERENCE TO MANUAL

WHAT THIS SCREEN IS ABOUT

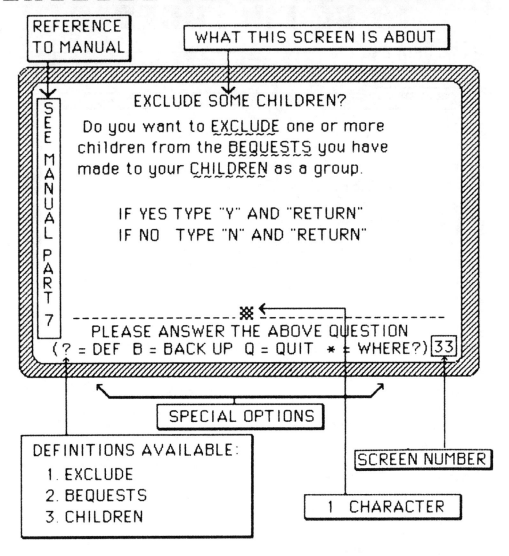

SEE MANUAL PART 7

EXCLUDE SOME CHILDREN?

Do you want to EXCLUDE one or more children from the BEQUESTS you have made to your CHILDREN as a group.

IF YES TYPE "Y" AND "RETURN"
IF NO TYPE "N" AND "RETURN"

PLEASE ANSWER THE ABOVE QUESTION
(? = DEF B = BACK UP Q = QUIT * = WHERE?) 33

SPECIAL OPTIONS

DEFINITIONS AVAILABLE:
1. EXCLUDE
2. BEQUESTS
3. CHILDREN

SCREEN NUMBER

1 CHARACTER

INDICATE CHILDREN
TO BE EXCLUDED

REFERENCE
TO MANUAL

WHAT THIS SCREEN IS ABOUT

SEE MANUAL PART 7

THE CHILDREN YOU HAVE NAMED:
1. GOODIE BUNNY
2. SUGARPLUM BUNNY
3. BLACKSHEEP BUNNY
4. SUNSHINE BUNNY
5. PRODIGAL BUNNY

   TYPE NUMBER OF CHILD TO EXCLUDE: ※...
WHEN LIST IS OK TYPE "Y" & "RETURN"

- -

34

DEFINITIONS AVAILABLE:
  1. *** none ***

2 CHARACTERS

SCREEN NUMBER

**EXAMPLE: If you type "3" & "Return" the screen will look like.:.......
You will have excluded Blacksheep Bunny.
Type "Y" when you are done with exclusions.
To restore Blacksheep, enter a "3" again.**

THE CHILDREN YOU HAVE NAMED:
1. GOODIE BUNNY
2. SUGARPLUM BUNNY
3. BLACKSHEEP BUNNY **X**
4. SUNSHINE BUNNY
5. PRODIGAL BUNNY

PERSONAL GUARDIAN

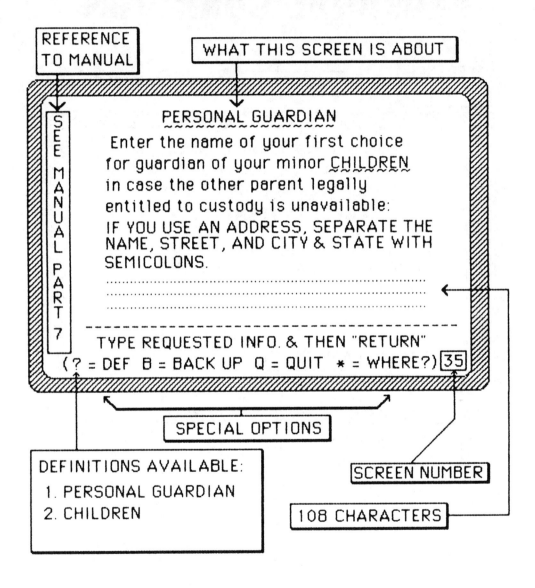

REFERENCE TO MANUAL

WHAT THIS SCREEN IS ABOUT

SEE MANUAL PART 7

PERSONAL GUARDIAN
Enter the name of your first choice
for guardian of your minor CHILDREN
in case the other parent legally
entitled to custody is unavailable:
IF YOU USE AN ADDRESS, SEPARATE THE
NAME, STREET, AND CITY & STATE WITH
SEMICOLONS.

TYPE REQUESTED INFO. & THEN "RETURN"
(? = DEF B = BACK UP Q = QUIT * = WHERE?) 35

SPECIAL OPTIONS

DEFINITIONS AVAILABLE:
1. PERSONAL GUARDIAN
2. CHILDREN

SCREEN NUMBER

108 CHARACTERS

169

ALTERNATE PERSONAL GUARDIAN

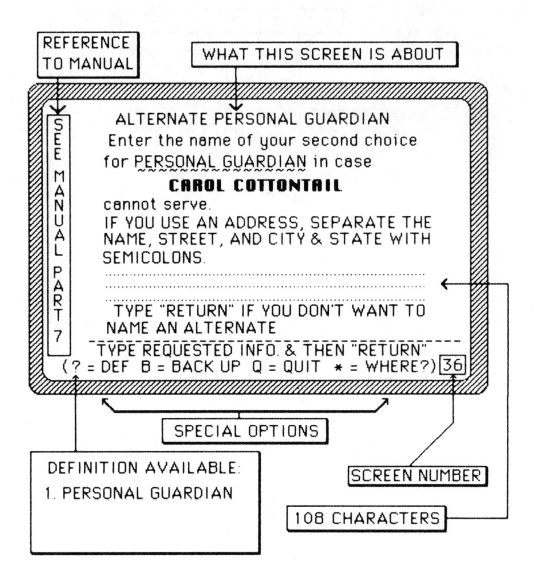

REFERENCE TO MANUAL

WHAT THIS SCREEN IS ABOUT

SEE MANUAL PART 7

ALTERNATE PERSONAL GUARDIAN
Enter the name of your second choice
for PERSONAL GUARDIAN in case
CAROL COTTONTAIL
cannot serve.
IF YOU USE AN ADDRESS, SEPARATE THE
NAME, STREET, AND CITY & STATE WITH
SEMICOLONS.
....
....
TYPE "RETURN" IF YOU DON'T WANT TO
NAME AN ALTERNATE
TYPE REQUESTED INFO. & THEN "RETURN"
(? = DEF B = BACK UP Q = QUIT * = WHERE?) 36

SPECIAL OPTIONS

DEFINITION AVAILABLE:
1. PERSONAL GUARDIAN

SCREEN NUMBER

108 CHARACTERS

GUARDIAN OF THE ESTATE

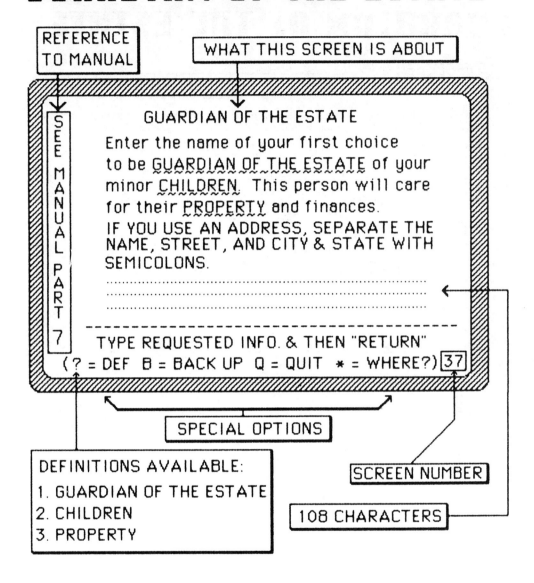

REFERENCE TO MANUAL

WHAT THIS SCREEN IS ABOUT

SEE MANUAL PART 7

GUARDIAN OF THE ESTATE

Enter the name of your first choice to be GUARDIAN OF THE ESTATE of your minor CHILDREN. This person will care for their PROPERTY and finances.
IF YOU USE AN ADDRESS, SEPARATE THE NAME, STREET, AND CITY & STATE WITH SEMICOLONS.

....
....
....

TYPE REQUESTED INFO. & THEN "RETURN"
(? = DEF B = BACK UP Q = QUIT * = WHERE?) 37

SPECIAL OPTIONS

DEFINITIONS AVAILABLE:
1. GUARDIAN OF THE ESTATE
2. CHILDREN
3. PROPERTY

SCREEN NUMBER

108 CHARACTERS

ALTERNATE
GUARDIAN OF THE ESTATE

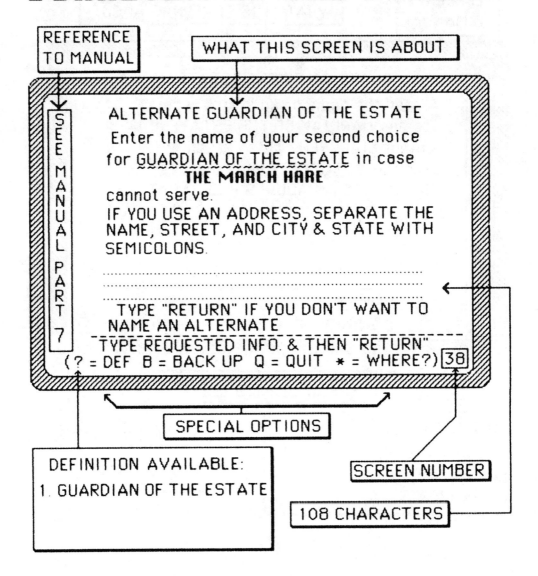

REFERENCE TO MANUAL

WHAT THIS SCREEN IS ABOUT

SEE MANUAL PART 7

ALTERNATE GUARDIAN OF THE ESTATE

Enter the name of your second choice
for GUARDIAN OF THE ESTATE in case
THE MARCH HARE
cannot serve.
IF YOU USE AN ADDRESS, SEPARATE THE
NAME, STREET, AND CITY & STATE WITH
SEMICOLONS.
....
....

TYPE "RETURN" IF YOU DON'T WANT TO
NAME AN ALTERNATE
TYPE REQUESTED INFO. & THEN "RETURN"
(? = DEF B = BACK UP Q = QUIT * = WHERE?) 38

SPECIAL OPTIONS

DEFINITION AVAILABLE:
1. GUARDIAN OF THE ESTATE

SCREEN NUMBER

108 CHARACTERS

172

EXECUTOR

REFERENCE TO MANUAL

WHAT THIS SCREEN IS ABOUT

SEE MANUAL PART 9

EXECUTOR

Enter the name of your first choice
to be EXECUTOR to see that your will
is carried out. (This can be someone
who receives property in your will.)

IF YOU USE AN ADDRESS, SEPARATE THE
NAME, STREET, AND CITY & STATE WITH
SEMICOLONS.

....
....
....

TYPE REQUESTED INFO. & THEN "RETURN"
(? = DEF   B = BACK UP   Q = QUIT   * = WHERE?) 39

SPECIAL OPTIONS

DEFINITION AVAILABLE:

1. EXECUTOR

SCREEN NUMBER

108 CHARACTERS

ALTERNATE EXECUTOR

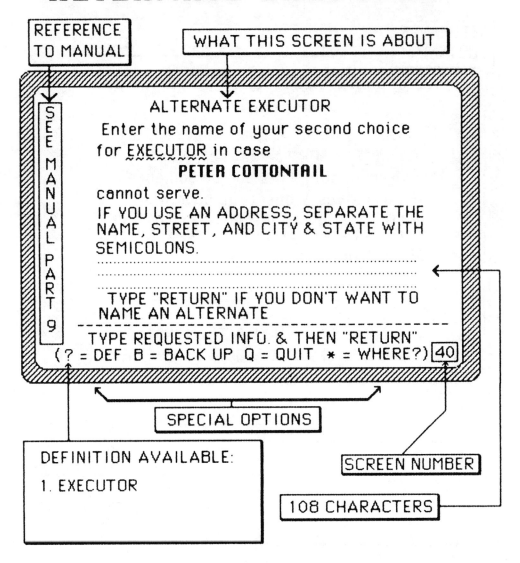

REFERENCE TO MANUAL

WHAT THIS SCREEN IS ABOUT

SEE MANUAL PART 9

ALTERNATE EXECUTOR

Enter the name of your second choice
for EXECUTOR in case
PETER COTTONTAIL
cannot serve.
IF YOU USE AN ADDRESS, SEPARATE THE
NAME, STREET, AND CITY & STATE WITH
SEMICOLONS.

....
....

TYPE "RETURN" IF YOU DON'T WANT TO
NAME AN ALTERNATE
- -
TYPE REQUESTED INFO. & THEN "RETURN"
(? = DEF B = BACK UP Q = QUIT ∗ = WHERE?) 40

SPECIAL OPTIONS

DEFINITION AVAILABLE:

1. EXECUTOR

SCREEN NUMBER

108 CHARACTERS

174

REVIEW/MODIFY

REFERENCE TO MANUAL

WHAT THIS SCREEN IS ABOUT

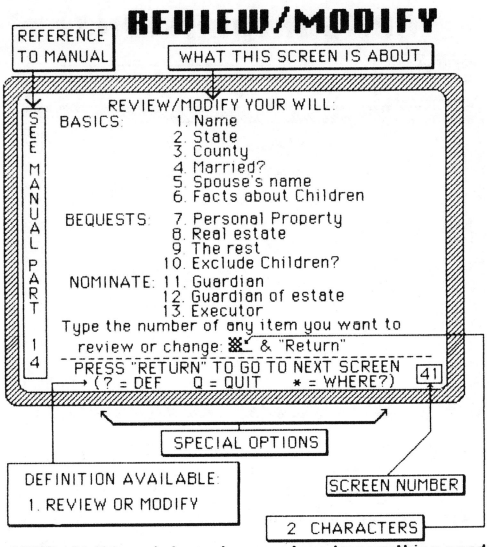

SEE MANUAL PART 14

REVIEW/MODIFY YOUR WILL:

BASICS:
1. Name
2. State
3. County
4. Married?
5. Spouse's name
6. Facts about Children

BEQUESTS:
7. Personal Property
8. Real estate
9. The rest
10. Exclude Children?

NOMINATE:
11. Guardian
12. Guardian of estate
13. Executor

Type the number of any item you want to review or change: ▓ & "Return"

PRESS "RETURN" TO GO TO NEXT SCREEN
(? = DEF   Q = QUIT   * = WHERE?)   41

SPECIAL OPTIONS

DEFINITION AVAILABLE:
1. REVIEW OR MODIFY

SCREEN NUMBER

2 CHARACTERS

NOTE: At this point you have entered everything needed for your will, but WillWriter gives you the chance to check the information. Simply type the number corresponding to the part you want to check (and then "Return"). If you make changes in some items you will come back to this screen directly after you make and verify the change. In some cases, the change affects other items in the will, and WillWriter takes you through a review of such items, and perhaps some new items.

CONGRATULATIONS

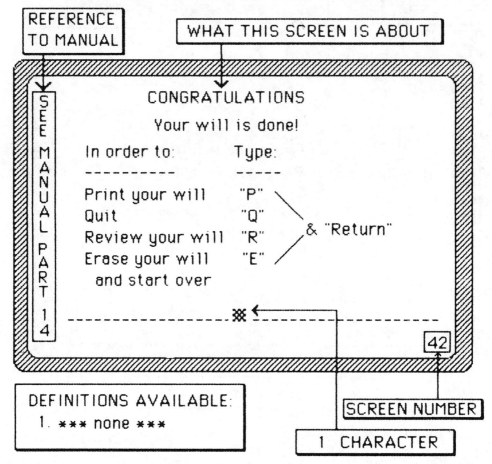

REFERENCE TO MANUAL

WHAT THIS SCREEN IS ABOUT

SEE MANUAL PART 14

CONGRATULATIONS

Your will is done!

In order to: Type:
----------   -----
Print your will   "P"
Quit   "Q"   & "Return"
Review your will   "R"
Erase your will   "E"
  and start over

※ ←

42

DEFINITIONS AVAILABLE:
1. *** none ***

SCREEN NUMBER

1 CHARACTER

NOTE: After you have finished your will, this is the main menu, and you will return to this screen every time you start up WillWriter. Use the Erase option only if you want to discard all of the will information stored on the diskette and start over from scratch. Review lets you look at all the information and make changes or corrections. Enter "P" to go to the print program, or "Q" if you want to save the information and quit.

K. IBM User's Notes

1. About Your IBM PC/XT/Pcjr Version of WillWriter

Your WillWriter diskette contains the Apple version on one side and the IBM version on the other. By IBM version we mean that the program was developed for the IBM PC, the IBM XT (essentially a PC with a built-in hard disk drive), and the PCjr (sometimes called the Peanut). The program should work on the IBM AT as well. See also the "IBM Compatibles Note" below.

In addition to one of these computers and the WillWriter diskette, you will need the following:

● The PC Disk Operating System (PC DOS version 2.0 or later), but see the "IBM Compatibles Note" below;

● IBM BASIC 2.0 (or later versions) or Advanced BASIC. IBM BASIC is available on a cartridge for the PCjr.;

● At least one floppy disk drive;

● A display screen (color or monochrome);

● Any printer that works with your computer;

● 128K of Random Access Memory.

The first two are software items that usually come with your computer system. The next three are hardware items that are also typically included in IBM products and compatibles. Some people do not purchase printers, however.

You can prepare your will without a printer but it has no legal effect unless it is printed out and signed in accordance with the formalities described in Part 11 of this manual. If you don't have a printer, you might consider running the program, getting your will in shape, saving it to the disk, and later printing it out at a friend's, or at an obliging computer store. WillWriter uses only the most basic of printing commands and will work with any printer that works with your computer.

IBM COMPATIBLES NOTE: Although WillWriter has been designed to run on the IBM products listed above, care has also been taken to make the program as system-independent as possible. Accordingly, WillWriter works just fine on any "IBM compatible" system that has 128K (some need 256K) or more RAM and can run IBM BASIC, Advanced BASIC, or the equivalent (including Compaq BASIC).

2. Copying Your WillWriter Diskette

Before you take even this initial step, you may want to make a copy of the WillWriter diskette for use and save your original for back-up purposes. To do this, follow the disk-copying procedures in your computer DOS manual.

If you have a hard disk, you may copy Will-Writer to it by issuing the following DOS command at your system prompt:
          Copy A:*.* C
or, if you have a directory called "Wills":
          Copy A:*.* C:/WILLS
Make sure you put a space between the last asterisk and the "C".

CAUTION: As we mentioned, your WillWriter diskette has an Apple version on one side and an IBM version on the other. This means that the diskette spins one way on the Apple and another on the IBM. If you switch the original Will-Writer diskette from an Apple to an IBM, or vice versa, you theoretically might encounter a dust problem in your drive.

Although this is highly unlikely, especially if you observe normal standards of cleanliness when handling the diskette, you would do better to initially use your copy and save your origin-al in case you ever want to switch Apple and IBM horses.

178

3. Getting WillWriter Up and Running

STEP A: Get the Disk Operating System (DOS) running by booting a system disk. Generally speaking, all you have to do is insert the system diskette in the disk drive, close the drive's door, and turn on the computer. Be sure the monitor is turned on as well. Consult your computer user's manual for details.

STEP B: Get BASIC running. On the PC, put a disk with your BASIC file (usually called BASIC.COM) in the drive, type the following string of characters:

BASIC/S:240 (BASICA/S:240 for users of Advanced BASIC)

and press the carriage return key. Then, remove your BASIC diskette, put in the WillWriter diskette, and type the following (with the quotation marks)

RUN "WW

and press the carriage return key. The program will then boot-up as described in Step C below.

For the PCjr., insert your BASIC cartridge and follow the procedure described above.

An alternative to this procedure is to copy your BASIC file (or Advanced BASIC file) onto the WillWriter diskette and proceed to Step C.

Step C: After copying BASIC (or Advanced BASIC) onto your WillWriter diskette, type WW (or WWA for Advanced BASIC) and press the carriage return key. After a few seconds you should see the WillWriter identification screen. The program will then proceed to the introductory section, where you will be told about wills and be given the opportunity to read instructions on the use of the program. We urge you to do so, at least the first time through.

STEP D: After the introductory screens are completed, there will be a short delay and then you will be off and running. If you decide to temporarily quit before you finish, simply press function key F2 (or type Q and press the "Return" key). Then, when you wish to resume the program, carry out these same steps and WillWriter will resume where you left off.

4. Special Features of the IBM Version

The major difference between the IBM version and the Apple version, aside from the color display, is that four of the special function keys are used to implement the following options which are available in the main part of the program.

• F1 is used to back-up to the previous logical section of the program (often, but not always, the previous screen). You can do the same thing by typing the letter B and then pressing the "Return" key, as in the Apple version.

• F2 is used when you need to stop working for awhile and you want to save your work on the diskette (or hard disk). You may also type the letter Q and press the "Return" key.

• F3 is used when you want to see definitions for one or more terms used on the screen (or sometimes a bit of advice). Alternatively, you can type the symbol ? and then press the "Return" key.

• F4 is used when you want to see exactly where you are in reference to the entire Will-Writer program. Your current location will be shown on a verbal map of the program. In addition to a "you are here" arrow, the earlier parts of the program which you have encountered will be marked with an "asterisk". The items without an asterisk have either not yet been reached or have been determined to be not relevant to your situation, on the basis of your earlier answers.

L. Commodore User's Notes

GETTING WILLWRITER UP AND RUNNING: Your first step should be to make a back-up copy of your diskette according to the Commodore procedures. Follow these instructions to get WillWriter running.

* Turn on the computer
* When screen says, "Ready", insert diskette
* Type the following command and then press Return (include quotation marks): Load "WW",8
* Screen will again say, "Ready". Type the following command and press Return: Run
* Program should begin operating

PART 15

Index of Legal Terms

ABATEMENT: The procedures used to distribute an estate when there is less property available for distribution than is given away in the will. See Part 8.

ADEMPTION: Cutting back certain gifts under a will when it is necessary to create a fund to meet expenses, pay taxes, satisfy debts, or to have enough to take care of other bequests which are given a priority under law or under the will. See Part 8.

ADOPTED CHILDREN: Any person, whether an adult or a minor, who is legally adopted as the child of another in a court proceeding. See Part 7, Section A.

ADULT: Any person over the age of 18. Most states allow all competent adults to make wills. A few, however, require you to be somewhat older (e.g., 19 or 21 to leave real estate). See Part 2. Competent adults may be left property without the need for appointing a guardian. See Part 2.

AUGMENTED ESTATE: A method used in a number of states following the common law ownership of property system to measure a person's estate for the purpose of determining whether a surviving spouse has been adequately provided for. Generally, the augmented estate consists of property left by the will plus certain property transferred outside of the will by such devices as gifts, joint tenancies and living trusts. In the states using this concept, a surviving spouse is generally considered to be adequately provided for if he or she receives at least one-third of the augmented estate. See Part 5, Section D.

BENEFICIARY: A person (or an organization) receiving benefits under a legal instrument such as a will or trust. Except when very small estates are involved, beneficiaries of wills only receive their benefits after the will is examined and approved by the probate court. Beneficiaries of trusts receive their benefits as provided in the trust instrument.

BEQUEST: As used in WillWriter and this manual, the personal property and real estate left to a person in a will. Thus, when you leave property to someone, you are said to make a bequest of that property.

BOND: A document guaranteeing that a certain amount of money will be paid to the victim if a person occupying a position of trust does not carry out his or her legal and ethical responsibilities. Thus, if an executor, trustee or guardian who is bonded (covered by a bond) wrongfully deprives a beneficiary of his or her property (say by taking it on a one-way trip to Las Vegas), the bonding company will replace it, up to the limits of the bond. Bonding companies, which are normally divisions of insurance companies, issue a bond in exchange for a premium (usually about 10% of the face amount of the bond). Under WillWriter, executors and guardians are appointed to serve without the necessity of purchasing a bond. This is because the cost of the bond would have to be paid out of the estate, and the beneficiaries would accordingly receive less. Under WillWriter, you should take care to select trustworthy people in the first place. See Part 9, Section A.

CASH BEQUEST: WillWriter permits you to leave specific personal property gifts to up to sixteen persons or institutions of your choice. These can be tangible property (i.e., tools, car, computer), intangible property (i.e., stocks, ownership of copyright or patent, pension), or straight cash. A gift consisting of cash is referred to as a "cash bequest." The cash for the cash bequest is raised by your executor, who is empowered to sell off property in the event the cash does not exist when you die. See Part 9, Section A.

CHILDREN: For the purpose of WillWriter, children are: 1) the biological offspring of the person making the will (the testator), 2) persons who were legally adopted by the testator, 3) children born out of wedlock if the testator is the mother, 4) children born out of wedlock if the testator is the father and has acknowledged the child as being his as required by the law of the particular state, or 5) children born to the testator after the will is made, but before his or her death. See Part 7, Section A.

CODICIL: A separate legal document that changes an existing will after it has been signed and properly witnessed. We do not recommend doing this. Because a codicil is subject to the same formal requirements as the original will, we suggest that if you wish to make changes, you use WillWriter to make a new will and then destroy your old one. See Part 12, Section B. Do not allow two wills to exist at the same time, as confusion about your intentions might result after your death. See Part 11.

COMMUNITY AND SEPARATE PROPERTY: Eight
states follow a system of marital property ownership called "community property." Very generally, all property acquired after marriage and
before permanent separation is considered to
belong equally to both spouses, except for gifts
to and inheritances by one spouse, and, in some
community property states, income property owned
by one spouse prior to marriage. See Part 5,
Section B for details.

In most marriages, the main property accumulated is a family home, a retirement pension
belonging to one or both spouses, motor vehicles, a joint bank account, a savings account,
and perhaps some stocks or bonds. So long as
these were purchased during the marriage with
the income earned by either spouse during the
marriage, they are usually considered to be
community property, unless the spouses have
entered into an agreement to the contrary.
If the property was purchased with the separate
property of a spouse, it is separate property,
unless it has been given to the community by
gift or agreement.

If separate property and community property
are mixed together (commingled) in a bank account and expenditures made from this bank account, the goods purchased will usually be
treated as community property unless they can be
specifically linked with the separate property
(this is called "tracing").

Under the law of community property states, a
surviving spouse automatically receives one-half
of all community property. The other spouse has
no legal power to affect this portion by will or
otherwise. Thus, the property which a testator
actually leaves by will consists of his or her
separate property and one-half of the community
property. To determine the net worth of an
estate, therefore, a spouse should add half of
the community estate (the sum total of the community property) to his or her separate property. See Part 5, Section B(1).

CONDITIONAL BEQUESTS: A bequest which only passes under certain specified conditions or upon the occurrence of a specific event. For example, if you leave property to Aunt Millie provided she is living in Cincinnatti when you die, and otherwise to Uncle Fred, you have made a "conditional bequest." WillWriter does not generally allow such conditional bequests. There is an exception, however. You can leave property to somebody on the condition that your primary beneficiary does not survive you by 45 days. Thus, you can leave your Leica camera to your friend Kenneth and then name Edith to receive the camera if Kenneth does not survive you by 45 days. You cannot, however, condition your bequest of the camera on Kenneth marrying your favorite niece. See Part 9, Section B.

DEVISE: An old legal term for real property that is transferred in a will. However, for ease of understanding, WillWriter uses the term "bequest" to refer to both personal and real property transfers by will.

DOWER AND COURTESY: The right of a surviving spouse to receive or enjoy the use of a set portion of the deceased spouse's property (usually one-third to one-half) in the event the surviving spouse is not left at least that share and chooses to take against the will. Dower refers to the title which a surviving wife gets, while Courtesy refers to what a man receives. Until recently, these amounts differed in a number of states. However, since discrimination on the basis of sex is now considered to be illegal in most cases, states generally provide the same benefits regardless of sex. See Part 5, Sections C and D.

ENCUMBRANCES: Debts (e.g., taxes, mechanic's liens, judgment liens) and loans (e.g., mortgages, deeds of trust, security interests) which use property as collateral for payment of the debt or loan are considered to encumber the property because they must be paid off before title to the property can pass from one owner to the next. Generally, the value of a person's ownership in such property (called the "equity") is measured by the market value of the property less the sum of all encumbrances. See Part 5.

ESTATE: Generally, the property you own when you die. There are different ways to measure your estate, depending on whether you are concerned with tax reduction (taxable estate--see Part 6, Section C), probate avoidance (probate estate--see Part 6, Section B), or net worth (net estate--see Part 5, Section H).

ESTATE PLANNING: The art of dying with the smallest taxable estate and probate estate possible while continuing to prosper when you're alive and yet passing your property to your loved ones with a minimum of fuss and expense. See Part 6, Sections C and D.

ESTATE TAXES: Taxes imposed by the federal government on your property as it passes from the dead to the living. The federal government exempts $400,000 of property in 1985, $500,000 in 1986 and $600,000 in 1987 and thereafter. Also, all property left to a surviving spouse is exempt under the marital exemption. Taxes are only imposed on property actually owned by you at the time of your death. Thus, estate planning techniques designed to reduce taxes usually concentrate on the legal transfer of ownership of your property while you are living, to minimize the amount of such property you own at your death. See Part 6, Section C.

EQUITY: The difference between the fair market value of your real and personal property and the amount you still owe on it, if any. See Part 5, Section G.

EXECUTOR/EXECUTRIX: The person specified in your will to manage your estate, deal with the probate court, collect your assets and distribute them as you have specified. If you die without a will, the probate court will appoint such a person, who is then called the "administrator" of your estate. It is common for married persons to name their spouse to this position. Also, however, it is a good idea to name two alternates to your original choice. See Part 9, Section A.

FINANCIAL GUARDIAN: See GUARDIAN OF THE ESTATE.

GIFTS: Property passed to others for no return or substantially less than its actual market value is considered a gift when the giver (called the "donor") is still alive, and a bequest, legacy or devise when left by a will. Any gift of more than $10,000 per year to an individual is subject to the Federal Estate and Gift Tax. A donor is required to take the Estate and Gift Tax credit for gifts over $10,000 and the amount of the credit thus used up will not be available when the donor dies. In other words, if enough property is given away in gifts over $10,000 during a donor's life, the full amount of the donor's estate may be subject to federal estate taxation. On the other hand, if gifts are kept within the $10,000 annual limit, the tax exemption available to the estate will not be adversely affected. See Part 6, Section C.

GUARDIAN OF THE ESTATE: The person or institution appointed or selected in your will to care for the property of a minor child. Usually, the same person will serve as guardian of the person and guardian of the estate. However, it is also possible to split these tasks. Under WillWriter, all property left to minors will be treated in accordance with the Uniform Gifts (or Transfers) to Minors Act as it has been enacted in each state. See Part 7, Section A.

GUARDIAN OF THE PERSON: An adult appointed or selected to care for a minor child in the event no biological or adoptive parent (legal parent) of the child is able to do so. If one legal parent is alive when the other dies, however, the child will automatically go to that parent, unless the best interests of the child require something different, or (in some states) the court finds the child would suffer detri-

ment. However, many parents wish to control who
will take care of their children if both parents
die or if the surviving parent is unfit or
doesn't wish to assume this responsibility.
WillWriter allows you to name up to three guardians in your will in ranked order of prefer-
ence. The probate court will then decide whether your choice of guardians should in fact be
honored, taking into account the best interests
of the children. Although the courts will normally honor your choice, there is no iron-clad
guarantee of this. Sorry. See Part 7, Section
A.

HEIRS: Persons who are entitled by law to
inherit your estate if you don't leave a will,
or any person or institution named in your will.

INTERVIVOS TRUSTS: See LIVING TRUSTS.

INTESTATE SUCCESSION: The method by which
property is distributed when a person fails to
leave a will. In such cases, the law of each
state provides that the property be distributed
in certain shares to the closest surviving relatives. In most states, these are a surviving
spouse, children, parents, siblings, nieces and
nephews, and next of kin, in that order. The
intestate succession laws are also used in the
event an heir is found to be pretermitted (i.e.,
not mentioned or otherwise provided for in the
will).

JOINT TENANCY: A way to take title to
jointly owned real or personal property. When
two or more people own property as joint tenants, and one of the owners dies, the other
owners automatically become owners of the deceased owner's share. Thus, if a parent and
child own a house as joint tenants, and the
parent dies, the child automatically becomes
full owner. Because of this "right of survivorship," a joint tenancy interest in property does
not go through probate, or, put another way, is
not part of the probate estate. Instead it goes
directly to the surviving joint tenant(s) once
some tax and transfer forms are completed.

Placing property in joint tenancy is therefore a common tool used in estate planning designed to avoid probate. However, when property is placed in joint tenancy, a gift is made to any persons who become owners as a result. Thus, if Tom owns a house and places it in joint tenancy with Karen, Tom will have made a gift to Karen equal to one-half the house's value. This may have gift tax consequences. See Part 6, Section B(3).

LEGACY: An old legal word meaning a transfer of personal property by will. For ease of understanding, WillWriter uses the term "bequest" to refer to both real property and personal property transfers by will.

LIVING TRUSTS: Trusts set up while a person is alive and which remain under the control of that person during the remainder of his or her life. Also referred to as "intervivos trusts," living trusts are an excellent way to minimize the value of property passing through probate. This is because they enable people (called "trustors") to specify that money or other property (called the "trust corpus") will pass directly to their beneficiaries at the time of their death, free of probate, and yet allow the trustors to continue to control the property during their lifetime and even end the trust or change the beneficiaries if they wish. See Part 6, Section B.

MARRIAGE: A specific status conferred on a couple by state. In most states, it is necessary to file papers with a county clerk and have a marriage ceremony conducted by authorized individuals in order to be married. However, in the thirteen so-called "common law marriage" states, you may be considered married if you have lived together for a certain period of time and intended to be husband and wife. These states are: Alabama, Colorado, District of Columbia, Georgia, Idaho, Iowa, Kansas, Montana, Ohio, Oklahoma, Pennsylvania, Rhode Island, South Carolina and Texas.

Unless you are considered legally married in the state where you claim your marriage occurred, you are not married for purposes of WillWriter. Accordingly, the person you may have lived with all of your life cannot inherit as your spouse. See Part 5, Section A.

MARITAL EXEMPTION: A deduction allowed by the federal estate tax law for all property passed to a surviving spouse. This deduction (which really acts like an exemption) allows anyone, even a billionaire, to pass his or her entire estate to a surviving spouse without any tax at all. This might be a good idea if the surviving spouse is young and in good health.

If the surviving spouse is likely to die in the near future, however, your tax problems will very likely be made worse by relying on the marital exemption. This is because the second spouse to die will normally benefit from no marital deduction, which means the combined estate, less the standard estate tax exemption, will be taxed at a fairly high rate. For this reason, many older couples with adequate resources do not leave large amounts of property to each other, but rather, leave it directly to their children so that each can qualify for a separate tax exemption. See Part 6, Section D.

MAXIMUM POTENTIAL PROBATE ESTATE: The total market value of all the property that would be in your probate estate before the application of avoidance techniques.

MINOR: In most states, persons under 18 years of age. A minor is not permitted to make certain types of decisions (e.g., enter into most contracts). All minors are required to be under the care of a competent adult (parent or guardian) unless they qualify as emancipated minors (in the military, married, or living independently with court permission). This also means that property left to a minor must be handled by a guardian or trustee until the minor becomes an adult under the laws of the state. See Part 7, Section A.

NET ESTATE: The value of all your property less your liabilities. See Part 5, Section G.

PRETERMITTED HEIR: A child (or the child of a deceased child) who is either not named or not provided for in a will. Most states presume that persons want their children to inherit. Accordingly, children, or the children of a child who has died before the person making the will (the "testator") who are not mentioned or provided for in the will are automatically given a share of the estate unless such children are specifically disinherited in the will. Will-Writer gets around this problem by providing every such child $1.00 in addition to any other gift. See Part 7, Section B.

PROBATE: The court proceeding in which: 1) the authenticity of your will (if any) is established, 2) your executor or administrator is appointed, 3) your debts and taxes are paid, 4) your heirs are identified, and 5) your property in your probate estate is distributed according to your will (if there is a will). Many people feel probate is a costly, time-consuming process which is best avoided is possible. Accordingly, instead of leaving their property in a will, they use a probate avoidance device, such as a joint tenancy, trusts (including savings bank, "living," insurance and testamentary trusts), life insurance, etc. See Part 6, Section B.

However, even those who believe it wise to leave property outside of a will generally also recommend using a will too. This is because a person could inherit or accumulate property shortly before death and not have time to create an alternative plan to pass it on. Also, a will can accomplish such tasks as naming an executor, guardian and trustee, in addition to leaving property. In some states, very small estates are exempt from probate even if a will is used. See Part 6, Section A.

PROBATE ESTATE: All of your property that will pass through probate. Generally, this means all property owned by you at your death less any property that has been placed in joint tenancy, a living trust, a bank account trust, or in life insurance. See Part 6, Section B.

PROBATE FEES: Because probate is so laden with legal formalities, it is usually necessary to hire an attorney to handle it. Under the law of some states, an attorney handling probate is entitled to be paid a percentage of the overall value of the probate estate (i.e., your maximum potential probate estate). This can often mean that the attorney will take a large chunk of the estate before it is distributed to the heirs. If, for example, your sole estate consists of your home, whose market value is $900,000, it is this figure which will be used to compute the probate fees, even though you may only have an equity of $200,000. In such a case, the fees might easily equal $20,000, or 10% of your actual estate. High probate fees is one good reason to engage in estate planning techniques designed to pass your property outside of your will. Part 6, Section B.

PROPERTY, PERSONAL AND REAL: All land and items attached to the land, such as buildings, houses, stationary mobile homes, fences and trees are considered as "real property" or "real estate." All property which is not "real property" is considered personal property. See Part 9.

PROVING A WILL: Getting a probate court to accept the fact after your death that your will really is your will. In many states this can be done simply by introducing a properly executed will. In others, it is necessary to produce one or more witnesses (or affidavits of such witnesses) in court, or offer some proof of the testator's handwriting. Having a will notarized usually allows the will to "prove" itself" without the need for witnesses or other evidence.

QUASI-COMMUNITY PROPERTY: A rule in Idaho and California that requires all property acquired by people during their marriage in other states to be treated as community property at their death in the event the couple has moved to one of these states. See Part 5, Section B.

REAL ESTATE: A term used by WillWriter as a synonym for "real property." See PROPERTY, PERSONAL AND REAL.

REAL PROPERTY: See PROPERTY, PERSONAL AND REAL.

RESIDUARY ESTATE: All the property contained in your probate estate except for property that has been left to specifically designated recipients. Thus, your residuary estate includes "the rest of your real estate" and the "rest of your personal property." See Part 9, Section A.

SEPARATE PROPERTY: See COMMUNITY AND SEPARATE PROPERTY.

SPECIFIC BEQUEST: As used in WillWriter, a bequest of a specific item, such as a car, a house, an amount of cash, or a family heirloom. See Part 9, Section A.

SPOUSE: In WillWriter, your spouse is the person to whom you are legally married at the time you sign the will. If you later remarry, you will need to make a new will if you wish to leave property to your new spouse. See Part 5, Section B.

TAKING AGAINST THE WILL: The ability of a surviving spouse to choose a statutorily allotted share of the deceased spouse's estate instead of the share specified in his or her will. In most common law property states, the law provides for a surviving spouse to receive a minimum percentage of the other spouse's estate (commonly between one-third and one-half). If the deceased spouse leaves the surviving spouse less than this in, or outside of, the will, the surviving spouse may elect the statutory share instead of the will provision (i.e., take against the will). If the spouse chooses to accept the share specified in the will, it is called "taking under the will." See Part 5, Sections C and D.

TAXABLE ESTATE: The portion of your estate that is subject to federal and/or state estate taxes. See Part 6, Section C.

TENANCY-IN-COMMON: A way of jointly owning property in which each person's share passes to his/her heirs. The ownership shares need not be equal. See Part 5, Section A.

TESTATOR: The person making the will.

TRUST: A legal arrangement under which one person or institution (called a "trustee") controls property given by another person for the benefit of a third person (called a "beneficiary"). The property itself is termed the "corpus" of the trust. WillWriter cannot be used to create a trust for the benefit of your surviving children. However, there are many ways to establish such a trust while you are still alive. See Part 6, Sections B and C.

UNIFORM PROBATE ACT: A series of statutes which attempt to standardize probate procedures and which have been enacted into law in approximately half the states. See Part 5, Section F.

UNIFORM GIFTS TO MINORS ACT: A series of statutes that provide standard guidelines for transferring property to minors. Enacted into law by most states, the Uniform Gifts (or Transfers) to Minors Act is used by WillWriter to govern how property left to minors will be handled. See Part 7, Section E.

WILL: A legal document in which a person states various wishes about what he/she wants done after his/her death.

About Legisoft

Legisoft was founded by attorney Bob Bergstrom and scientist Jeffrey Scargle in the belief that personal computers are a natural and beneficial means of furthering the self-help law movement. Starting with a program that produced a form will good only in California, Legisoft soon realized that a more flexible and powerful will could be produced that would be valid nationwide. Will-Writer is the result. Legisoft is now devoted to producing additional high quality legal software for the personal computer and, in particular, developing computer programs which can easily incorporate the numerous changes inherent in the legal process.

About the Illustrator

Mari Stein is a freelance illustrator and writer. Her published work has been eclectic, covering a wide range of subjects: humor, whimsy, health education, juvenile, fables and Yoga. This is her fifth collaboration with Nolo Press; she has illustrated 29 Reasons Not To go To Law School, Author Law and Strategies, Media Law and How to Copyright Software. She works out of a studio in her Pacific Palisades home, where she lives with her dogs and rabbits, cultivates roses and teaches Yoga.

Business and Finance

How To Form Your Own California Corporation

By attorney Mancuso. Provides all the forms, Bylaws, Articles, minutes of meeting, stock certificates and instructions necessary to form your small profit corporation in California. Includes a thorough discussion of the practical and legal aspects of incorporation, including the tax consequences.

California Edition	$24.95
Texas Edition	$21.95
New York Edition	$19.95

The Non-Profit Corporation Handbook

By attorney Mancuso. Includes all the forms, Bylaws, Articles, minutes, and instructions you need to form a non-profit corporation. Step-by-step instructions on how to choose a name, draft Articles and Bylaws, attain favorable tax status. Thorough information on federal tax exemptions, which groups outside of California will find particularly useful.

California only $24.95

The California Professional Corporation Handbook

By attorneys Mancuso and Honigsberg. In California a number of professions must fulfill special requirements when forming a corporation. Among them are lawyers, dentists, doctors and other health professionals, accountants and certain social workers. This book contains detailed information on the special requirements of every profession and all the forms and instructions necessary to form a professional corporation.

California only $24.95

Billpayers' Rights

By attorneys Honigsberg and Warner. Complete information on bankruptcy, student loans, wage attachments, dealing with bill collectors and collection agencies, credit cards, car repossessions, homesteads, child support and much more.

California only $10.95

The Partnership Book

By attorneys Clifford and Warner. When two or more people join to start a small business, one of the most basic needs is to establish a solid, legal partnership agreement. This book supplies a number of sample agreements with the information you will need to use them as-is or to modify them to fit your needs. Buyout clauses, unequal sharing of assets, and limited partnerships are all discussed in detail.

National Edition $17.95

Plan Your Estate: Wills, Probate Avoidance, Trusts and Taxes

By attorney Clifford. Comprehensive information on making a will, alternatives to probate, planning to limit inheritance and estate taxes, living trusts, and providing for family and friends. Explains new California statutory will and includes actual forms.

California Edition	$15.95
Texas Edition	$14.95

WillWriter - a software/book package

By Legisoft. Use your computer to prepare and update your own valid will. A manual provides help in areas such as tax planning and probate avoidance. Runs on Apple II, II+, IIe, IIc and the IBM PC.

National Edition $39.95

The Power of Attorney Book

By attorney Clifford. Covers the process which allows you to arrange for someone else to protect your rights and property should you become incapable of doing so. Discusses the advantages and drawbacks and gives complete instructions for establishing a power of attorney yourself.

National Edition $14.95

Chapter 13: The Federal Plan to Repay Your Debts

By attorney Kosel. This book allows an individual to develop and carry out a feasible plan to pay most of his/her debts over a three-year period. Chapter 13 is an alternative to straight bankruptcy and yet it still means the end of creditor harassment, wage attachments and other collection efforts. Comes complete with all necessary forms and worksheets.

National Edition $12.95

Bankruptcy: Do-It-Yourself

By attorney Kosel. Tells you exactly what bankruptcy is all about and how it affects your credit rating, property and debts, with complete details on property you can keep under the state and federal exempt property rules. Shows you step-by-step how to do it yourself; comes with all necessary forms and instructions.

National Edition $14.95

Legal Care for Your Software

By attorney Remer. Shows the software programmer how to protect his/her work through the use of trade secret, trademark, copyright, patent and, most especially, contractual laws and agreements. This book is full of forms and instructions that give programmers the hands-on information they need.

International Edition $24.95

The Dictionary of Intellectual Property Law

By attorney Elias. "Intellectual Property" includes ideas, creations and inventions. This book focuses on the computer field, and provides functional and contextual definitions for the hundreds of law-related words and phrases commonly used in high technology commerce.
National Edition $19.95

How to Copyright Software

By attorney Salone. Shows the serious programmer or software developer how to protect his or her programs through the legal device of copyright.
International Edition $21.95

Small-Time Operator

By Bernard Kamoroff, C.P.A.. Shows you how to start and operate your small business, keep your books, pay your taxes and stay out of trouble. Comes complete with a year's supply of ledgers and worksheets designed especially for small businesses, and contains invaluable information on permits, licenses, financing, loans, insurance, bank accounts, etc. Published by Bell Springs.
National Edition $9.95

Start-Up Money: How to Finance Your Small Business

By Michael McKeever. For anyone about to start a business or revamp an existing one, this book shows how to write a business plan, draft a loan package and find sources of small business finance.
National Edition $17.95

The Patent Book

By attorney Pressman. Complete instructions on how to do a patent search and file a patent in the U.S. Also covers the simple procedure for filing a U.S. patent if one has already been granted in another country. Tear-out forms are included.
National Edition $21.95

Family and Friends

How to Do Your Own Divorce

By attorney Sherman. Now in its tenth edition, this is the original "do-your-own-law" book. It contains tear-out copies of all the court forms required for an uncontested dissolution, as well as instructions for certain special forms.
California Edition $12.95
Texas Edition $12.95

The Living Together Kit

By attorneys Ihara and Warner. A legal guide for unmarried couples with information about buying or sharing property, the Marvin decision, paternity statements, medical emergencies and tax consequences. Contains a sample will and Living Together Contract.
National Edition $14.95

California Marriage and Divorce Law

By attorneys Ihara and Warner. This book contains invaluable information for married couples and those considering marriage or remarriage on community and separate property, names, debts, children, buying a house, etc. Includes prenuptial contracts, a simple will, probate avoidance information and an explanation of gift and inheritance taxes. Discusses "secret marriage" and "common law" marriage.
California only $14.95

Sourcebook for Older Americans

By attorney Matthews. The most comprehensive resource tool on the income, rights and benefits of Americans over 55. Includes detailed information on social security, retirement rights, Medicare, Medicaid, supplemental security income, private pensions, age discrimination, as well as a thorough explanantion of the new social security legislation.
National Edition $12.95

After the Divorce: How to Modify Alimony, Child Support and Child Custody

By attorney Matthews. Detailed information on how to increase alimony or child support, decrease what you pay, change custody and visitation, oppose modifications by your ex. Comes with all the forms and instructions you need. Sections on joint custody, mediation.
California only $14.95

A Legal Guide for Lesbian/Gay Couples

By attorneys Curry and Clifford. Here is a book that deals specifically with legal matters of lesbian and gay couples: raising children (custody, support, living with a lover), buying property together, wills, etc. and comes complete with sample contracts and agreements.
National Edition $17.95

How to Adopt Your Stepchild

By Frank Zagone. Shows you how to prepare all the legal forms; includes information on how to get the consent of the natural parent and how to conduct an

"abandonment" proceeding. Discusses appearing in court and making changes in birth certificates.
California only $17.95

Rules and Tools

The People's Law Review
Edited by Ralph Warner. This is the first compendium of people's law resources ever published. Contains articles on mediation and the new "non-adversary" mediation centers, information on self-help law programs and centers (for tenants, artists, battered women, the disabled, etc.); and articles dealing with many common legal problems which show people how to do-it-themselves.
National Edition $8.95

Author Law
By attorneys Bunnin and Beren. A comprehensive explanation of the legal rights of authors. Covers contracts with publishers of books and periodicals, with samples provided. Explains the legal responsibilities between co-authors and with agents, and how to do your own copyright. Discusses royalties, negotiations, libel and invasion of privacy. Includes a glossary of publishing terms.
National Edition $14.95

Legal Research: How to Find and Understand the Law
By attorney Elias. A hands-on guide to unraveling the mysteries of the law library. For paralegals, law students, consumer activists, legal secretaries, business and media people. Shows exactly how to find laws relating to specific cases or legal questions, interpret statutes and regulations, find and research cases, understand case citations and Shepardize them.
National Edition $12.95

The Criminal Records Book
By attorney Siegel. Takes you step-by-step through the procedures available to get your records sealed, destroyed or changed. Detailed discussion on your criminal record--what it is, how it can harm you, how to correct inaccuracies, marijuana possession records and juvenile court records.
California only $12.95

Tenants' Rights
By attorneys Moskovitz, Warner and Sherman. Discusses everything tenants need to know in order to protect themselves: getting deposits returned, breaking a lease, getting repairs made, using Small Claims Court, dealing with an unscrupulous landlord, forming a tenants' organization, etc. Sample Fair-to-Tenants lease and rental agreements.
California Edition $9.95
Texas Edition $6.95

Everybody's Guide to Small Claims Court
By attorney Warner. Guides you step-by-step through the Small Claims procedure, providing practical information on how to evaluate your case, file and serve papers, prepare and present your case, and, most important, how to collect when you win. Separate chapters focus on common situations (landlord-tenant, automobile sales and repair, etc.).
National Edition $10.95
California Edition $9.95

Media Law: A Legal Handbook for the Working Journalist
By attorney Galvin. This is a practical legal guide for the working journalist (TV, radio and print) and those who desire a better understanding of how the law and journalism intersect. It informs you about censorship, libel and invasion of privacy; how to gain access to public records, including using the Freedom of Information Act; entry to public meetings and courtrooms; dealing with gag orders.
National Edition $14.95

How to Change Your Name
By attorneys Loeb and Brown. Changing one's name is a very simple procedure. Using this book, you can file the necessary papers yourself, saving $200 to $300 in attorney's fees. Comes complete with all forms and instructions for the court petition method or the simpler usage method.
California only $14.95

Homestead Your House
By attorney Warner. Under the California Homestead Act, you can file a Declaration of Homestead and thus protect your home from being sold to satisfy most debts. This book explains this simple and inexpensive procedure and includes all the

forms and instructions. Contains information on exemptions for mobile homes and houseboats.
California only $8.95

Your Family Records: How to Preserve Personal, Financial and Legal History
By Pladsen and attorney Clifford. Helps you organize and record all sorts of items that will affect you and your family when death or disability occur, e.g., where to find your will and deed to the house. Includes information about probate avoidance, joint ownership of property and genealogical research. Space is provided for financial and legal records.
National Edition $12.95

Fight Your Ticket
By attorney Brown. A comprehensive manual on how to fight your traffic ticket. Radar, drunk driving, preparing for court, arguing your case to a judge, cross-examining witnesses are all covered.
California only $12.95

Marijuana: Your Legal Rights
By attorney Moller. Here is the legal information needed to guaratee constitutional rights and protect privacy and property. Discusses what the laws are and how they differ from state to state.
National Edition $9.95

Write, Edit and Print
By Donald McCunn. Word processing with personal computers. A complete how-to manual including: evaluation of equipment, four fully annotated programs, operating instructions and sample applications.
525 pages. $24.95

Computer Programming for the Compleat Idiot
By Donald McCunn. An introduction to programming your P.C. in BASIC. Hardware and software are explained in everyday language and the last chapter gives information on creating original programs.
$10.95

Murder on the Air
By Ralph Warner and Toni Ihara. An unconventional murder mystery set in Berkeley, California. When a noted environmentalist and anti-nuclear activist is killed at a local radio station, the Berkeley violent crime squad swings into

action. James Rivers, an unplugged lawyer, and Sara Tamura, Berkeley's first female murder squad detective, lead the chase. The action is fast, furious and fun. $5.95

29 Reasons Not to Go to Law School
A humorous and irreverent look at the dubious pleasures of going to law school. By attorneys Ihara and Warner, with contributions by fellow lawyers and illustrations by Mari Stein. $6.95

How to Become a United States Citizen
By Sally Abel. Detailed explanation of the naturalization process. Includes step-by-step instructions from filing for naturalization to the final oath of allegiance. Includes a study guide on U.S. history and government. Text is written in both English and Spanish.
National Edition $9.95

The Landlord's Law Book: Rights and Responsibilities
By attorney Brown. Covers the areas of discrimination, insurance, tenants' privacy, leases, security deposits, rent control, liability, and rent withholding.
California only $19.95

Landlording
By Leigh Robinson (Express Press). Written for the conscientious landlord or landlady, this comprehensive guide discusses maintenance and repairs, getting good tenants, how to avoid evictions, record keeping and taxes.
National Edition $15.00

The Eviction Book for California
By Leigh Robinson (Express Press). Here are suggestions for preventing evictions and, if that fails, instructions for scrupulous landlords/landladies who want to handle evictions themselves for nonpayment of rent, breach of contract, waste, nuisance, unlawful acts or failure to vacate. Forms included.
California only $14.95

Order Form

Quantity	Title	Unit Price	TOTAL

Prices Subject to change

☐ Please send me a catalogue

Tax: (CA only; San Mateo, LA, Santa Clara & BART counties, 6 1/2%; all others, 6%)

Name _____

Address _____

_____

___ VISA ___ Mastercard

_____ exp. _____

Signature _____

Phone ( ) _____

Subtotal _____

Tax _____

Postage & Handling _____

TOTAL _____

Credit card information or a check may be sent to NOLO PRESS, 950 Parker St., Berkeley, CA 94710 or call (415) 549-1976

OR

Send a check only to NOLO DISTRIBUTING, Box 544, Occidental, CA 95465

Specifications

Requirements:

>   Apple: A 64k,II+, IIe, or IIc
>
>   IBM: PC, XT, PCjr, and true compatibles.
>   PC DOS 2.0 or later, Basic (or Advanced
>   Basic) 2.0 or later. When loading Basic,
>   type Basic/S:240
>
>   Commodore 64 & 128 "128 with emulation mode"
>   Apple: 64K RAM
>
>   IBM: 128K RAM
>   (some compatibles need 256K RAM)
>
>   One disk drive
>
>   A display device
>
>   Any standard printer that works with the
>   computer

Operating System:

>   ProDOS (Apple) - supplied with the disk
>   Nothing required for Commodore
>   PC DOS (IBM) and Basic - not supplied
>   with the disk

Languages: Basic and Assembly

WillWriter can be copied to a back-up diskette or
to a hard disk.

All editing must be done through the program
rather than another editing program.

WillWriter is a rule-based system using abstact
data structures and a blackboard.

Copy Protection:

WillWriter is not copy protected